The Good Sleep Guide

for you and your baby

An____son

Hawthor.

Published by Hawthorn Press, Hawthorn House,
1 Lansdown Lane, Stroud, Gloucestershire, GL5 1BJ, UK
Tel: (01453) 757040 Fax: (01453) 751138
E-mail info@hawthornpress.com
Website www.hawthornpress.com

Cover photograph by Mary Alliston
Cover design and typesetting by Bookcraft Ltd, Stroud, Gloucestershire
Printed by The Cromwell Press, Trowbridge, Wiltshire
Printed on acid-free paper from managed forests

Reprinted 2003; 2004

British Library Cataloguing in Publication Data applied for

ISBN 1 903458 35 8

IMPORTANT NOTICE TO PARENTS/CARERS

This guide is intended as a summary of established British medical practice on baby sleep promotion techniques at the time of publication. The guide has been widely recommended by UK health visitors and has been used successfully by thousands of parents without professional help, but using it without medical supervision is at your own risk. The author is a researcher, not a medical practitioner, and can take no responsibility for any harm or mishap befalling your baby while following the advice in this guide, nor for any changes in standard medical practice that take place subsequent to the purchase of any one individual copy. **A baby sleep programme such as that in sections 5 and 6 of this guide is best used with the help of your health visitor and should not be carried out before the child is six months old; you must also check with a medical practitioner first if you have any concerns about your baby's health.** Those using the guide outside the UK should understand that any issues arising from its use would only be dealt with within the context of the British legal system.

Contents

Special note for US readers

Some words used frequently in the text are not used in the USA. The translation guide below explains English terms:

UK	USA
Dummy	Pacifier
Cot	Crib
Nappy	Diaper
Breast-feed (to)	Nurse (to)
Pushchair	Stroller

Foreword

Helping families with the repercussions of ongoing infant sleep problems is one of the most recurrent and time-consuming areas of my work, as it is for other health visitors. Associated parental sleep deprivation has long been recognised as a major cause of unwanted disruptions to family life – liable to lead, if not dealt with, to problems which can include: relationship/marriage breakdown, failure to bond with the child, physical and mental health problems and other undesirable consequences. The stressful environment caused by lack of a predictable sleep routine can also affect the child, in time leading to erratic feeding patterns which may affect growth and development in general. The frustrating thing about such situations is that most sleep disturbances in babies can be either easily prevented or cured at an early stage.

Parents using this invaluable sleep guide frequently tell me how thrilled and surprised they are at the ease with which long-standing problems are resolved with its help – sometimes in just a few days.

I fully recommend this unique guide for a variety of reasons. Firstly, its concise step-by-step format is far more appropriate for exhausted parents than other more lengthy books (which can appear overwhelming), or the brief leaflets sometimes available from health professionals (which may not give detailed enough guidance to ensure real change.) Despite being concise, it is comprehensive and gets to the 'nub' of the issues – it is simply the best baby sleep guide available!

Secondly, it is easy to use and a well-researched summary of clinically-approved techniques, rather than yet another new theory. Health visitors can therefore safely rely on it to provide an ideal back-up for work with both individuals and groups. For this reason it has become established with thousands of health visitors as the Number One baby sleep resource. The presentation is very clear and the 'signed agreement' section will be particularly useful in reinforcing parental commitment to carry out this programme. The sleep diary at the end of this guide is also an essential tool.

Thirdly, *The Good Sleep Guide* has been successfully tried and tested over five years by parents who know this approach works. This second edition has been updated with feedback from these parents as well as from health professionals.

Prevention is clearly better than cure – and this is why I recommend that parents read *The Good Sleep Guide* before or as soon as possible after the birth of a baby. The updated prevention section in this new edition is really excellent. By educating yourself in good time about the nature of baby sleep patterns, what is realistic to expect from your child at different ages, and most importantly, how best to respond to your child's needs at night, you will have the best possible chance of enabling your baby to develop sound sleeping habits.

For parents already experiencing problems, the easy quiz format is an excellent aid to identifying which of a wide range of possible contributory factors may be relevant in their case. This approach ensures, before you start on a full baby sleep programme, that other possible causes of sleeplessness, including dietary, physical and emotional factors, are fully addressed.

If you are already having sleep problems, your chances of success are greatest if you follow this guide with health visitor support. And for new parents, it is my hope that forewarned and forearmed, you really can prevent problems occurring and hence look forward to many sleep-filled nights.

Joan Wood, RN, RM, ONC, RSCN, RHV
Corsham Family Health Centre, August 2002

Author's introduction

'Does your baby sleep through the night?' is one of the most common questions new parents get asked, and the topic most often discussed amongst parents themselves. We glow with pride when we can say: *She is really good at night.*[1] We may almost feel a sense of failure if we cannot say this – as though we lack parenting ability, or as if our child is to blame in some way. Desperate for sleep and with the best of intentions, many parents end up spending hours each night, often for months on end, helping their babies settle back to sleep – and as a result often feel exhausted, confused and lacking guidance on this important subject.

With my first baby, Amber, despite my degree in psychology and a wide range of books on childcare, I was also confused. Although she had slept through the night at four months, she started waking frequently again at 6 months. Totally exhausted from sleep deprivation and having just resumed a demanding job, I was at the end of my tether. One day I had half an hour for a much-needed walk on my own to clear my head: in the chemist I overheard a mother asking for drugs to get her child to sleep. Horrified, I realised that though this was a tempting option, I would never resort to such methods. Wandering bleary-eyed into my local bookstore, I caught sight of a book – *Teach Your Baby to Sleep Through the Night.* On the back cover it promised me a good night's sleep in only three to seven days if I changed my night-time strategies. I did; and in three days, thankfully, we were both enjoying a full night's sleep.

After that experience I developed a personal passion for this subject. When my second baby, Joseph, was born four years later, I decided to use my time at home with him to research and write the first edition of this book. I wanted to produce the truly concise and easy-to-follow guide I had so needed myself the first time around. My research confirmed what I suspected after my success with Amber: that despite one or two areas of controversy, there were tried and tested methods being used by health professionals and in clinics, but that this knowledge was often not getting through efficiently to sleep-deprived parents.

---

1   To avoid the awkward use of both genders throughout, I will alternate she and he from chapter to chapter.

Don't worry if you are too tired to focus on the page, let alone read a whole book! The structure of this book is very simple:

- Sections 1–2 help you identify if you have a problem.
- Sections 3–4 help avoid a problem developing for younger babies, and give suggestions on where your baby should sleep.
- Sections 5–6 are for parents of babies over 6 months who still wake regularly at night. These sections prepare for and outline a 'Baby Sleep Programme' to help your baby develop independent sleeping habits.
- Section 7 focuses on frequently asked questions and the help section provides a further reading list and useful contact addresses should you need further help or support.
- The Appendices are separate from the main text, as optional reading for those who need more information on certain topics (such as weaning, the role of food allergies or coping with crying).

I wanted the thousands of parents known to be suffering (needlessly) night after night to be able to avoid going through this. This guide, therefore, does not claim to contain any new 'miracle cure', merely to summarise in an easily accessible way what is already known by clinicians, used by health visitors, and proven to work.

It is now five years since this book was first published, and I am thrilled to say, judging from the huge number of letters I receive from relieved and delighted readers, that writing it has been one of the most rewarding things I have ever done. This new edition incorporates comments and case histories from such letters, as well as valuable tips from parents and health visitors. Keep those letters coming please, via Hawthorn Press (address at front of book), with comments, results, details of any other books, papers or relevant organisations you have come across on this subject. Your comments and experiences can be used to enrich future editions.

I still meet many mothers who do not realise, as I did not, that the way parents behave can affect a baby's behaviour. It is easy to become defensive and protective about the strategies we develop to cope with our child's sleep patterns, not wishing to discuss the matter or take any further advice. But there is no need to be ashamed: it is understandable that so many of us are confused about how best to meet our babies' needs. We live in a time when society and child-rearing practices are changing so radically and so quickly that we have become confused, losing the natural confidence which previous generations had in dealing with their babies. The babies become as confused as we are – no wonder they cannot develop sound sleep patterns. First-born babies have more sleep problems than subsequent ones, presumably because parents are usually more confident about what to do the second time around. This guide will help you to create consistent and appropriate routines which will give you back a feeling of being in control as a parent.

Although this book has been written especially for parents, I know that it has also become extremely popular with health professionals. It is strongly recommended that parents develop a good relationship with their health visitor, who can help and support them in carrying out these suggestions. It is also recommended that both partners/parents read this book – new approaches will work better and more successfully when supported by the whole family. If you wish to buy this guide in quantity, to distribute amongst parents or local groups, please contact the publisher direct. If you have ideas for topics that future health guides should cover, then do also let us know.

Take courage – these techniques do work. I hope that this book will help you either prevent or cure the nightmare of sleep deprivation that so many new parents have to endure unnecessarily. The first few months with a new baby should be a time of joy for the whole family, and this book can help ensure that it is.

Angela Henderson
Forres, Scotland, August 2002

1

What is 'sleeping through'?

It's been a hard day's night, and I been working like a dog,
It's been a hard day's night, I should be sleeping like a log ...
John Lennon and Paul McCartney

About your baby's sleep pattern

Before we look at what is 'normal' and when you can expect your child to 'sleep through the night', it is useful to understand more about the nature of babies' sleep patterns and the difference between baby and adult sleep.

There are two basic types of sleep for both babies and adults:

- deep or 'slow wave' sleep (in which it is hard to wake the sleeper, the body is very relaxed, no dreaming occurs); and
- a shallower 'rapid-eye-movement' or REM sleep (in which dreaming and eye-and-body movements occur, and from which we wake easily).

As adults we spend the majority of our sleeping time in deep sleep and although we may stir or even wake as we pass from deep to REM sleep, in general we do not remember this. **Babies spend far more time than adults in shallow sleep, and are much more easily woken.**

'Sleeping through' the night

When filmed sleeping, 80 per cent of babies are seen waking and opening their eyes for short periods. So we should know that it is completely natural for babies to wake frequently for brief periods at night. How you react to this natural night waking, after a certain stage has been reached, is crucial in determining whether your baby will learn independent sleeping habits later on.

> Your sleep is disrupted when your child cries for *your help* to go back to sleep rather than putting *himself* back to sleep when waking naturally at night.

A baby who 'sleeps through the night' is therefore a baby who, while still waking naturally at night, does not cry for help to go back to sleep and can sleep unaided for an acceptable period.

How much do babies sleep?

The US Center for Pediatric Sleep Disorders estimates that:

- **at 1 month** a typical baby sleeps a total of 15 hours per day: nearly 9 hours at night and the rest divided into three daytime naps;
- **by 3 months** nearly 10 hours at night and 5 hours during the day;
- **by 6 months** 11 hours at night and just over 3 hours during the day in two naps;
- **by 9 months** gradually more at night and less during the day; until
- **by 1 year** you can expect 11½ hours at night on average, followed by just over 2 hours sleep during the day in two naps.

Please bear in mind that these are *averages* of *total sleep with interruptions*, and in practice extremely variable.

What can I expect from my baby?

Be realistic with newborns   There is controversy about when babies 'should' start sleeping through the night – and how long for. It is important to be realistic about what is achievable in terms of *unbroken* night-time sleep, particularly with a newborn baby. Sometimes I get letters from new mothers with very young babies, asking me if I can help them with their 'sleep problem' as they need to get a good night's sleep in order to return to their jobs. Sadly, in such cases the parent's expectations of what their baby is capable of are simply unrealistic. (If you are planning to return to work whilst your baby is under 6 months of age, do read Appendix 5.)

It is important to be aware that the constant day and night feeding demands of most newborns are inevitably going to lead to some disruption of sleep for those providing the feeds, usually the mother. However, there are ways of minimising this disruption at night. Research shows that choices about day and night-time feeding routines and frequency, the baby's sleeping environment, how you behave with your baby at different stages of development and other factors, all affect whether your newborn will develop good sleep habits or not. Section 2 will help you decide whether or not you already have a 'problem' sleeper.

What experts say is possible

- **3-month-old babies**   The current research definition of normal 'sleeping through' is a baby who, by 12 weeks of age, sleeps at least five hours of unbroken sleep between the hours of midnight and 7 am. (Five hours sleep without a break may not seem a lot to a tired parent, but it may comfort you to know that this is seen as normal at this age.)
- **6-month-old babies**   American experts seem to agree that babies should be able to sleep at least nine unbroken hours by 6 months, although some UK experts feel this is over-optimistic

What actually happens

But if your baby is not sleeping through, take heart, you are not alone! Results from the ongoing *Avon Longitudinal Study of Parents and Children* (ALSPAC – see references), the largest ever UK survey of its kind, of nearly 14,000 families, reveal figures that are startling to those who know how easy it can be to use sleep-promoting methods such as those explained in this guide.

According to these results, a third of parents of 6-month-old babies are up between one and eight times each night engaged in a variety of soothing behaviours: rocking/cuddling, feeding and giving dummies were reported as the most common solutions. Many experts believe that these figures are higher than they need to be. This book will help you understand why such behaviour is totally appropriate for a newborn baby, but how it can become counterproductive if these active soothing strategies are continued past the newborn phase.

Most experts in the fields of medicine and psychology agree that by 6 or 7 months a baby can *learn* to sleep unaided for most of the night even if he has not already done so without help.

SUMMARY

- It is natural for babies to wake more frequently at night than adults
- Most newborn babies (0–12 weeks) will need regular feeds throughout the night.
- A 3-month-old baby can only be expected to sleep for one 5-hour stretch at night without a feed, though some will sleep for longer than this.
- A 6-month-old baby can learn to sleep unaided for most of the night, even if he has not already done so without help.

2

Do we have a problem?

What hath night to do with sleep?
Milton *Comus*, 1.122

What is a 'sleep problem'?

Psychologists report wide variation in how parents perceive what a problem is. Some inexperienced parents are horrified by even half an hour of crying or the very fact of night feeding during the first weeks. Others will put up with almost anything.

A situation is only a problem if you find it problematic, and the aim of this book is not to make you feel guilty about what you are doing if everyone is happy with it. However, it is worth knowing what the long-term consequences of your current routines might be. What does not seem a problem at 7 months (e.g. lying down next to your baby for half an hour while she goes to sleep every evening) may well seem a problem when you have to go on doing it for several years, or if your young child does not let a babysitter replace you!

Defining what a 'problem' is, is difficult. However, the founders of 'The Crying Baby Clinic' in the USA, have attempted to create definitions in this elusive area. They define a child with a sleep problem as:

An infant who does not have a regular sleep/wake pattern of 9 hours' consecutive sleep during the night by 6 months of age, and who wakes up more than 3 nights per week for more than one month. They also define a child with a problem as: *A tired child who takes over 30 minutes to fall asleep on her own* – when this pattern continues for over a month.

Does my baby have a problem?

Your baby would not normally be thought a problem if she is under 6 months of age and still waking up at night – as long as she is sleeping a sufficient number of hours in total. However, if she seems to you to be sleeping unusually few hours overall, do get professional help or use the methods in this guide to encourage her into longer periods of sleep. (The advice in Section 3 will help you with babies of this age). To decide whether your *baby of 6 months or more* has a 'problem', you may find these questions helpful:

- Does she sleep for significantly fewer hours at night than the average for her age? (see guidelines on page 2)
- Is she unable to fall asleep without my physical presence (feeding, rocking, stroking, etc)?
- Does she wake and cry for me regularly in the night?
- Is my work/health/relationship/family being negatively affected by sleep deprivation?

If you answer 'yes' to two or more of these, then you can certainly benefit by following the baby sleep programme in Sections 5 and 6 of this guide. Section 3 contains the keys you need to encourage your younger baby into independent sleeping and will help you avoid the need for a more structured sleep programme later on. (Don't worry if your child is older than 6 months; the programme can be started at any point up to 18 months of age, although it may take longer to succeed with older babies.)

Results from the ALSPAC study found that

- 33.1% (one third) of children at 6 months were waking up either most nights or every night; and
- 49.5% (nearly half) were waking regularly once or more per night at 18 months of age.

This would seem to indicate that ensuring your baby is encouraged into good sleep habits from the start will help avoid having a wakeful toddler later on.

How do problems start?

'She did sleep well, but now she wakes ... '

Some babies start off sleeping through the night as newborns, but then their sleep patterns deteriorate. This can occur for a variety of reasons, many of them unavoidable:

- an illness, teething or a period of colic;
- a major change in routine such as moving house.

Other factors listed in the literature as being linked to sleep disruption in young babies include stressful events in pregnancy, particularly difficult births, premature or low birth weight babies and parental stress. However, knowing what caused your problem does not necessarily bring about a cure!

How we can make things worse

The factors listed above are largely unavoidable. But there is one important thing that we can change and control and that is the way we parents behave with our baby. We naturally tend to sooth a newborn baby through rocking, making certain sounds, holding her and providing movement which calms crying. One writer, Dr. Harvey Karp (see page 23 and further reading section) believes that the reason newborn babies all seem to respond so well to these things is because certain kinds of noise, touch and motion mimic the womb environment. This provides helpful 'extra womb time' for babies who are necessarily 'evicted' from the womb somewhat early, before their heads are too big to get through the birth canal.

As these things work so well for a newborn baby, the natural tendency as parents, particularly when we are in a state of sleep deprivation, is to cling desperately to any routines and tactics which have worked in the past. As a result we can find ourselves still needing to perform such activities with a ten-month-old. By continuing these, we are actually training our child to need them after a certain age, so that she cannot fall asleep without them! One thing this guide will show you is how to wean your child off these things and hence not cry for you at night.

> On many occasions I ended up driving around with her in the car at 3am and then trying to sleep in the car myself once she was asleep!
>
> *Katherine Davis, Bath*
>
> James at 13 months woke at least twice each night and had to be rocked to sleep in our bed. We felt desperate.
>
> *Rhianwen Gilson, Wiltshire*
>
> I used to have to lie down on the bed next to Jonathan, sometimes for hours, just to get him to go to sleep.
>
> *Mrs. Clarke, Staffs.*

Sleep deprivation – a health warning

There are two main reasons for avoiding or curing a sleep problem. The first is to protect the physical and emotional well-being of you and your whole family. If your baby is not sleeping, then either or both parents will be sleep-deprived. Effects of long-term sleep deprivation listed in the literature include: disorientation, weight loss, chronic fatigue, irritability, depression, broken marriages and child abuse. There are cases where individuals already predisposed to illnesses such as ulcers and diabetes have developed these through the long-term stress of living with a night crier. Sleep deprivation is so debilitating that it has been used in prison camps and in cult programming to destroy the ability to think and concentrate.

> We were both a wreck. Our production at work suffered and we even missed days due to no sleep. We were so exhausted that we were irritable and just all around miserable.
>
> *Angela Brewer, Spokane, USA*
>
> I was finding it increasingly difficult to cope with my other child, 2-year-old Melissa. I felt as if my baby was in charge, not me. I had forgotten what it was like to feel rested and refreshed.
>
> *Maree White, Bath*

What is important is to have a period of uninterrupted sleep, not several hours of broken sleep. When parents are at the 'end of their tether' this can create a stressful and chaotic environment for the child's early development. And if, as in some extreme cases, the situation contributes to your relationship actually breaking up, this is obviously far from ideal for the child.

The second reason for avoiding sleep deprivation is to further the child's own physical and emotional well-being. Broken nights and the tiredness these produce will interfere with your baby's mood and feeding routines and will ultimately affect her physical and psychological development. Babies and children who find it hard to sleep may also end up with sleep problems as adults.

> Holly (now 10 months) never slept during the day and averaged 4–5 hours broken sleep at night. I looked and felt exhausted and near to the edge of a nervous breakdown. Both she and our poor 2-year-old had to put up with a grumpy, edgy mummy most of the time.
> *Natasha Radford, Essex*

Take action now!

If, having read this chapter, it has become clear to you that you have a sleep problem, it is important to take action soon, especially if you and your family are all suffering from the side-effects of sleep deprivation. If you postpone taking action because it seems easier in the short term, you will only find the problem harder to remedy later on.

If you do nothing, sleep problems *may* improve on their own, but it could take many months or even years.

A reader's advice

Don't put off trying to tackle the problem (as we did), it just gets more difficult. Remember it is much better for your child as well as for you that they learn how to sleep happily.

Rhianwen Gilson, Wiltshire

SUMMARY

- A third of 6-month-old babies still always or usually wake at night, but this can often be prevented.
- Sleep deprivation can have serious effects on your health, well-being and family life.
- If you maintain early soothing strategies into older babyhood you may prolong night-waking.
- It is always best to take action sooner rather than later – things tend to get worse.

3

Six keys to good sleep for you and your (younger) baby

Sleep, that knits up the ravelled sleeve of care ...
W. Shakespeare   *Macbeth*

This section offers you tried and tested ways to help your baby learn independent sleeping habits – certainly by the 5/6 month stage and hopefully much earlier. There are a few 'miracle sleepers' (one study showed that only 4 per cent of babies *never* woke at night at 4 weeks!), but it is important to be realistic about what your young baby is capable of. Although, as we shall see, many young babies often wake more regularly at night than is necessary, some night waking for one or more feeds is inevitable in the early weeks.

If you are finding the challenge of new parenthood quite a task, you are not alone. One study in the year 2000 showed that it costs the NHS £65 million annually to provide support for parents coping with infant crying and sleeping issues from birth to 12 weeks! If you are a mother or main carer particularly eager for your baby to 'sleep through', as you are considering returning to work outside the home, see Appendix 5 which provides extra tips on how to help ease this transition.

The two most important features underlying these keys are: establishing clear routines and learning how best to respond to your baby at his different stages of development.

Six keys to good sleep at night

1 Create a clear difference between night and day.
2 Provide a private, peaceful sleeping place.
3 Let your baby learn to settle himself.
4 Have regular daytime feeding and sleeping routines.
5 Naturally minimise night-time feeding.
6 Keep things calm and predictable in the evening.

KEY ONE

Create a clear difference between night and day

Myth   *Babies don't know the difference between night and day*

In University studies, one favoured strategy for promoting good sleep is to teach parents to create a clear difference between their approach to night-time and day-time. Although it is true that babies tend to replicate at night what they experience in the day, feeding regularly throughout both, you can quite quickly begin to teach them the difference.

The sleeping environment

Create a difference between day-time naps and night-time sleeps by making sure your bedroom or the nursery is kept as dark as possible at night, and is naturally lighter in the daytime. Use the minimum of light for night-time feeds; never put the overhead light on. In general, keep the sleeping environment quiet and undisturbed at night (for instance, take things out at bed-time which you may need during the evening). If possible, avoid having your newborn baby share a room with noisy older children until his sleeping habits are really well established.

Do not 'fuss' your baby at night

Once he is settled, try hard not to over-check or disturb him. If you follow the safety advice in Section 4, there will be less need to worry about your baby when he is asleep. Use a baby monitor to hear if he starts crying and try not to go in otherwise.

Learn to distinguish between real cries and sleep noises

Your baby will naturally reach a lighter level of sleep at intervals and may, at this time, gurgle or make other sleep noises. Do not respond immediately to your baby when these occur, only to full blown cries.

Do not interact socially with your baby at night

When feeding at night, behave very differently from a day-time feed. Keep quiet, do not talk to him or interact 'socially'. Make it clear that night is for sleeping, not for playing. Change nappies only when really necessary and also in relative silence.

Introduce a small time delay before feeding

When you feel able, but certainly by 3 months of age, start introducing a short period of delay between his first little cries for a night feed and the actual feed. If you wish to keep crying to a minimum, you can still offer other reassurance such as stroking and soothing noises.

Our newborn baby Joshua weighed 9 lbs 3 ozs which I thought would lead automatically to good sleep! But I learned that sleep has nothing to do with a baby's birth weight and everything to do with habit.
Marrianne and Lee Beaumont, Oxon

I actually started following many suggestions in your guide at about 3 months and by 5 and a half months she was sleeping 12 hours a night and a couple in the day. She is one of the most contented babies and falls asleep within seconds of being put in her cot.
Vanessa Impey, Glasgow

> ## Interacting with your baby at night-time
>
> - Do not respond to 'night noises', only real cries.
> - Keep the nursery as dark and quiet as possible.
> - Do not talk or interact socially with your baby.
> - Only change a nappy if completely necessary.
> - By 3 months, introduce a small time delay between the cry and the feed.

KEY TWO

Provide a private, peaceful sleeping place

Myth   *Make the nursery more interesting and baby will like going to bed*

A peaceful sleeping place

Experts agree that many parents make the fundamental mistake of making the cot or crib and the nursery 'over-stimulating'. It is common to find new parents-to-be shopping excitedly for all the latest 'cot toys': mobiles involving music, lights, sounds and a plethora of other decorative items. Bedtime is about peace, quiet and sleep – not about play – so save your money!

A private sleeping place

It is a good idea to create a cosy, private sleeping place right from the start, even if it is only used for part of the night and for some daytime naps. Most babies do not start their sleeping career in their eventual big cot, but move into this from about 3 months onwards. (The ALSPAC survey showed that only 12.5 per cent of 1-month-old babies are put down in a cot to sleep at night, with 79 per cent being put down in a cradle, carry cot or Moses basket). Very small babies tend to prefer smaller and warmer 'nests' to start with.

Statistics show that most mothers initially have the cradle, cot or basket in their own bedroom. Usually for ease of feeding, the vast majority of mothers (77.1 per cent in this study) choose to *room-share* (but not necessarily *bed-share*) in the early weeks. This room-sharing policy is also endorsed by the

Foundation for the Study of Infant Death (FSID) as the best strategy for avoiding 'cot death' or Sudden Infant Death Syndrome (SIDS). (For more on this, see Section 4.)

In the same study, a total of 64.6 per cent of mothers reported taking their young babies into their bed at least sometimes (with about a quarter doing this usually or always). Whether or not to bed-share is a much-debated issue and very much your own choice. Section 4 offers the pros and cons of both short and longer-term bed-sharing, and provides important safety information for any parent planning to bed-share with their baby even occasionally.

Getting your baby used to the cot

The ALSPAC survey found that by 6 months of age, 65.2 per cent of parents have moved their babies into a separate nursery, with only a third still sleeping in the mother's bedroom. I certainly found that, despite bed-sharing initially, I was beginning to need some personal space by the time my baby was 6 months old – and more importantly, I felt my baby was ready for hers.

Wherever he sleeps at night early on, I recommend that you give your baby *some* experience of sleeping alone and privately as early as possible, and by 3 months at the latest. This will make it much more likely that he will be happy with this as his only sleeping place when he is older, if this is what you wish.

These same principles apply to getting a smaller baby used to the crib or cradle if he usually sleeps in your bed.

Tips for acclimatising your baby to his cot

- Put your baby into his cot for some of his daytime sleeps.
- Always put your baby into the cot if he is sleepy.
- Once he is used to it, start using it at night, especially if it is in your own room.

KEY THREE

Let your baby learn to settle himself

Myth   *If you find a technique which works to get him to sleep, stick to it*

With very young babies, particularly those who suffer from 'colic' and have long crying periods (for more on this see Key Six), most parents' priority is understandably to develop soothing and settling strategies which enable their babies to fall asleep. I remember my tiny baby feeding and falling asleep at my breast and it was a wonderful experience. Other common strategies include movement (rocking), touch (stroking) and other methods that mimic the womb environment. Some desperate parents resort to driving the baby around in the car. One parent even reported beating a drum!

However, there comes a point, as your baby grows, at which these rituals become counterproductive 'sleep associations'. The child will associate the act of falling asleep with them, growing less and less able to fall asleep without them. As adults we all have sleep habits – such as needing to sleep on one side or the other, sleeping with a certain pillow, sleeping better in our own bed, etc. Although we probably don't cry when unable to do so, we may feel like it if we cannot sleep! Babies are the same in this respect. Once your baby has grown used to these soothing rituals he will cry if they are not forthcoming, in the middle of the night too: the very thing which initially cured his night crying will actually cause more.

At this stage it is really important for your baby to learn to put himself to sleep – and for you to be freed from hours of involvement with these soothing habits! In general, the longer they persist, the harder they are to break. Some people who let them endure until the 6-month stage may encounter far more resistance during a baby sleep programme, if required after this stage, than if they gradually introduced good habits earlier on.

> Bad sleeping habits are confusing for the child. You have taught him that he needs your help to fall asleep; but then, when he wakes naturally at night and needs your help to go back to sleep, you may respond with some annoyance (or at least feel it!).

As soon as you can, it is important to put your baby down in his sleeping place awake, for both day-time and night-time sleeps.

Put your baby down to sleep awake

This is probably the single most important piece of advice in this whole book, so take note! Babies who can put themselves to sleep when they wake naturally in the night are known technically as 'self-soothing'. When we as adults wake up in the night we lie in our beds until we drift back to sleep. If your baby has never done this, he has to learn how to do it and we need to give him the chance to do so.

He will certainly tolerate this from 3 months onwards, and even earlier. Use your soothing techniques – such as feeding, stroking, singing, etc. – as part of your pre-bed routine, and if at all possible try not to let him fall asleep at the breast.

Tips for teaching 'self-soothing' (ideally by 3 months)

- Put your baby to bed *awake*, as young as possible.
- To start with, try doing this for daytime sleeps, whilst staying close.
- Tickle his foot to keep him *awake* if he starts to fall asleep while feeding.
- Remember, a little whimpering now is better than hours of screaming later.

If he starts sleeping through – don't stop him!

This may seem a crazy statement, but sometimes parents inadvertently interfere with their babies' efforts to develop a period of unbroken sleep. Many people find that at the age of about one month their baby will suddenly sleep for an unbroken period of 5–6 hours, when previously he was waking up every 2–3 hours. If this happens to your baby once he is a month old or more, make a careful note of exactly which hours he managed to sleep between. He has now shown you that he is capable of sleeping, without a feed, for this period. Respect this now as his main sleep period and follow the instructions below.

Tips for reinforcing longer, unbroken, night-time sleep periods

- Aim not to feed or pick him up again during this period.
- Ideally, put him in his cot or separate sleeping place for this period.
- If he whimpers or grizzles during this time, leave him alone if possible.
- If he starts crying, slightly delay your response and calm with non-feeding methods.

Joshua would fall asleep at the bottle and so wanted the same thing to get back to sleep again during night wakings. Your guide helped me understand how this habit, and our mistake of letting him fall asleep in our arms and not in his cot, had started at birth. From waking twice per night for long periods, our son now sleeps 11 hours at night.

Marrianne and Lee Beaumont, Oxon

KEY FOUR

Have regular daytime feeding and sleeping routines

Myth   *Breast-fed babies should be 'demand fed' as often as you/they wish*

Some childcare experts tend to favour the idea of 'demand feeding' for breast-feeding mothers as good for establishing milk supply and for soothing newborn babies. However, an important new study from the Thomas Coram Research Unit in London (see references) has found that, at 1 week, babies who feed extremely frequently – more than 11 feeds in 24 hours or an average of every two hours or less – are nearly three times more likely to fail to sleep through the night by 12 weeks of age than those babies who feed less frequently. In addition, other experts point out that extremely frequent breast-feeding on demand can cause sore nipples and lead to exhausted mothers who may ultimately be put off breast-feeding completely.

> Night waking is affected by how often feeds occur during the day. Babies in general initially replicate the daytime feeding schedule at night, so if they are fed very frequently in the day they will expect the same at night.

If a baby takes longer than 40 minutes for a feed, he is usually a 'sucky' baby who is sucking at the nipple for comfort after the feed has finished. You should try to gradually reduce the length of the feed and find other ways to comfort him once the feed is finished (putting your finger in his mouth is one strategy). Only give dummies as a last resort to such babies, as they can reduce the success of breast-feeding; or just use them sparingly in the evenings.

Tips for daytime feeding under 3 months

- Aim to create a daytime feeding routine which is the same each day.
- 'Sucky' babies may be using the nipple as a dummy.
- Try to soothe such babies in other ways. Only use dummies as a last resort.
- If feeds are 2 hours apart or less, increase the interval between feeds by 15 minutes each time until feeds are nearer 3 hours apart.

This last point is perhaps less realistic for the early evening period when you are tired, your milk supply is low and your baby may need more frequent feeds to be satisfied. If you are finding it hard to achieve a suitable daytime feeding routine, please do get professional help from your health visitor or an NCT breast-feeding counsellor (see the help section). See also the passage on 'growth spurts' at the end of this section.

Daytime sleeping routines

Myth   *If I keep my baby awake in the day he will sleep better at night*

Night sleep can be affected when babies over a year old sleep too much in the day, but this does not apply to young babies. With newborns, sleep should be treated as a habit – in many ways: *the more they do it the better at it they get*! If your young baby does not get enough sleep in the daytime, not only may his feeding and development be affected, but he will actually take longer to settle at night as he will be grizzly and fretful and unable to enjoy his bed-time routine.

How much should he sleep in the day?

Babies vary in the number and length of daytime naps they have and obviously you need to develop a schedule which fits in with your life. Once your baby has settled into a day-time sleeping routine, it should ideally be a priority to stick to it as far as possible as this will help him develop a routine of good night-time sleep. At 1 month your baby will probably need about 6 hours of daytime sleep, by 3 months this may fall to about 4–5 hours and by 6 months to 3–4 hours. This should be divided into 2–3 sleep periods.

Where should he sleep in the daytime?

Many parents like at least one of the daytime sleeps to be outside in a pram or reclining buggy. Experience shows us that babies often sleep well outside in the fresh air, provided they are in a safe, private place and well wrapped up. They also love looking at the moving leaves on the trees above them!

But it is also important to use the daytime naps to get your baby used to his own private sleeping space (see Key Two), so maybe do at least one of each. Try to avoid making a nap in the car or carry chair a regular feature (although we all do it sometimes!). You may make it harder for him to settle at night in his cot.

Waking up a napping baby

Whenever possible, try to let him wake up on his own, rather than waking him up, and if you have to wake him, do so gradually and gently by partly waking him and then letting him 'come to' on his own. It has been suggested that if we repeatedly wake a napping baby in a rushed or sudden way then he may develop a habit of becoming instantly alert when he half wakes, instead of remaining drowsy and drifting back to sleep.

> ## Tips for daytime sleep routines
>
> - Tired babies will take *longer* to settle at night.
> - Respect the daytime routine once it is established.
> - Use daytime naps to help him get used to his cot.
> - Let him wake naturally if possible.

KEY FIVE

Naturally minimise night-time feeding

Myth   *If my baby cries at night, he must need feeding*

We have seen how babies can become dependent upon the things that happen just before they fall asleep, and the importance of putting them down to sleep awake. We have also discussed the importance of responding differently during the day and at night. By following the advice of all the previous keys, you should find that your baby's need for night feeds will reduce naturally.

Phasing out night feeds from 4 months

There may be a 'growth spurt' at approximately 3 months, and certainly by 4 months you can further help your baby reduce the night feeds if he has not already done so naturally. (If your baby was premature, he may not be ready until a little later.) Certainly a healthy baby should no longer need a night feed after 5 months. If you need help with weaning your baby off night feeding, see Appendix 1. Unnecessary night feeding, given after there is no longer a physical need for food, places undue stress on the digestive system and will prevent the development of proper sleeping habits.

The late evening feed

University researchers trying to establish how best to encourage babies to 'sleep through' generally agree that if possible you should establish a 'focal feed' between 10.00–12.00 pm – just before you go to bed. Many baby-care experts also think there should ideally be a feed at this time, until the age of about 5 months. This enables babies to have their main chunk of unbroken sleep (which might only be 5 hours initially) between that last feed and 5 am, allowing parents at least a small stretch of unbroken sleep themselves.

In practice, this can be difficult to achieve if your baby is generally fast asleep at this time, as you may be rightly reluctant to wake a sleeping baby. In theory, if you have put your baby to bed early enough (say at 7pm), then he should be ready for a feed at this time; but if you have kept him up, for whatever reason, he may not be. You could try experimenting and see if a feed (in a dimly lit room with a minimum of social interaction) helps or hinders the rest of his nightly routine. If you need more in-depth advice on the timing of feeding routines, I suggest you consult *The Contented Little Baby Book* (see further reading section).

If you are a mother-to-be who is absolutely dreading the thought of night feeds during the first few months after birth, there is some small comfort: there is evidence that breast-feeding biologically alters mothers' sleep cycles, enabling them to wake more naturally in response to their infant. In addition, pregnant women often notice night waking increasing naturally prior to delivery, in preparation for the baby.

Tips for night feeding under 3 months

- Newborn babies will generally wake 1–3 times a night for a feed.
- Each feed should last 10–30 mins.
- If longer or more frequent seek help from your health visitor or NCT breast-feeding counsellor.
- One method is to gradually delay the response time at night by a few minutes (stroke or cuddle, rather than allowing to cry).

KEY SIX

Keep things calm and predictable in the evening

Myth   *There is not much you can do about colicky evening crying except wait for him to 'grow out of it'*

'Why is he crying?' must be one of the most frequent pleas of new parents! To hold a baby, sometimes for hours on end, while he cries, can be exhausting and demoralising.

It is not necessarily easy to learn to understand our baby's needs in the first few months. He may cry a lot in the first few weeks – and one of the things we try to learn as parents is whether he is hungry, uncomfortable, ill, colicky, releasing tension or over-stimulated. Babies cry in an aversive and grating manner to assure an immediate response from you, his parents. It may be some small comfort to you, if your baby cries a lot, that crying has some side benefits and is not necessarily bad for him.

Crying can be

- the beginning of the ability to vocalise;
- good exercise that strengthens heart and muscles;
- most importantly, a way of releasing stored up distress and tension.

Newborn to 3 months: avoiding 'colic' and evening crying

Nobody really knows what 'colic' is and what causes it. It is a term used to describe 3-week to 3-month-old babies' tendency to cry, often for long periods (usually from 1 to 3 hours), and almost always in the evening. Theories abound as to its cause: the result of an immature digestive system, trapped wind from over-enthusiastic feeding, a sensitivity to cow's milk formula, breast-feeding mothers eating the wrong foods, and so on. Certainly, in some cases, resolving the issues above can ease crying. (See Appendix 4 on diet if you suspect food allergy and page 61 for advice on foods to omit from the diet of breast-feeding mothers.)

However, the most convincing explanation I have come across for this mystery condition, is from Dr. Harvey Karp. He is convinced that the chief reason why young babies cry so much in the evening is that, in terms of development, human babies are born very prematurely compared with other mammals and that their immature brains simply cannot cope with overstimulation in our modern world. If tension is built up in the daytime, it has to be released in the evenings. For this reason, he argues, to keep this evening crying at a minimum, we must keep our homes as quiet and calm as possible. This can often be a chaotic, stressful time: a parent might be just home from work, the TV on in the background, meals to cook and possibly friends calling in. Try turning the TV off (excessive TV can distress small babies), get yourself as calm as possible, put some quiet music on, perhaps discourage visitors at certain evening times, and devote yourself instead to soothing your baby. To read more fully about the soothing techniques, see Dr. Karp's own book: *The Happiest Baby* (listed in further reading section).

I believe that by enabling your baby to release his stored-up tension effectively in the evenings – without creating new stress around him when *he* needs to release tension – you will achieve better sleep at night. If you find it hard to do this or if you become very stressed by either evening or night-time crying, please turn to Appendix 2 for ways to help you cope with it.

Strategies to calm 'colicky' crying in the evenings (birth to 3 months)

- Keep your home calm, quiet and visitor-free.
- Give your baby your full attention while he cries.
- Try not to let his cries make *you* more stressed.
- Massage, stroking, rocking and calm music may help soothe your baby.

The importance of bed-time routine

As part of your calm evening period, introduce a bed-time routine from about 2 months of age. Babies love such a routine – which is why it is good if they have slept well in the day, so that all of you have the energy to create and enjoy it. Try not to rush it or miss 'bits' of it out. Make the routine predictable, at the same time every day, at least 30–60 minutes before the bed-time you have chosen for your baby (which will be somewhere between 6–8 pm).

The routine can include: stories, bath-time, changing into special night-time clothes, lullabies, baby massage – ending with the last feed. **Use your soothing techniques as part of this routine, but remember to put your baby down to sleep *awake*.**

A note about 'growth spurts'

There are frequent reports of otherwise settled babies suddenly becoming more clingy, crying more, feeding more frequently and sleeping less at regular stages in the first year. Some experts think that this is not due to physical growth, but because the baby is learning new skills. The leaps in development are in some ways stressful to the baby and he needs more reassurance and possibly more food at these 'regression periods'. Try not to give up with breast-feeding if these occur – if you 'weather the storm' he will soon settle again and the mother's milk production may actually be stimulated by extra demand. 'Growth spurts' may be expected at 5 weeks, 8/9 weeks, 12 weeks, 15–19 weeks and 23–26 weeks.

4

Where should my baby sleep?

There is another evil attending the sleeping together of the mother and infant ...
that most injurious practice of letting the child suck after the mother has fallen
asleep ... she wakes languid and unrefreshed from her sleep.
Mrs. Beeton's Book of Household Management, 1861

Should I bed-share with my baby?

This extract from a well-known guide to Victorian household management may seem a little extreme to us, but it gives an interesting insight into the fact that there was as much disagreement in Mrs. Beeton's day about whether mothers should share their bed with their babies as there is today! Although it has been a common practice throughout history, this debate has reportedly been going on for many centuries: there are even records of 13th Century Bishops instructing their clergy to urge mothers not to sleep with their babies, in order to prevent suffocation. Today there is still scientific disagreement about whether the benefits of this ancient practice outweigh the new risks caused by bed-sharing in our modern sleeping environments.

This section will:

- provide some important safety information on baby sleeping places;
- air the pros and cons of the 'family bed versus cot' controversy.

Possible effects upon your child's future sleeping habits will also be considered.

As we have seen, most mothers choose to put their new babies to sleep in a small cradle, cot or Moses basket in their bedroom, at least for the first few months – then move them later into their own bedroom. The majority of mothers sometimes have their babies in bed with them, at least occasionally, during the early weeks.

My personal experience of early bed-sharing

When my own babies were newborn, my instinct, like that of many other mothers, was to keep them as physically close to me as possible for as long as I felt right – night and day. When my first baby was born I kept her in my bed both in the hospital and when we returned home – something we both very much enjoyed.

During that time I came across various books which fascinated me and very much supported my initial decision. These included Jean Liedloff's well-known book, *The Continuum Concept,* which compares our childcare practices in the western world with those of South American Indians. The author's observation was that the babies of tribal people very rarely cry, always sleep with their parents or other family members, and are generally carried physically on the mother's body until they are ready to crawl away of their own accord. I also learned that in Europe until the 19th century, and in many other parts of the world today, mothers still routinely sleep with their babies (see further reading section). My own baby also seemed to be much happier by day when strapped more or less constantly to me in a sling.

However, by the time she was 3 months old I was beginning to need some personal space. So I gradually moved her from my bed (via a Moses basket next to the bed) into a cot in an adjoining room. In addition, I was beginning to develop back problems from the strain of carrying my very heavy baby day after day! I began to suspect that different theories were probably appropriate for babies at different ages and stages of development. I also felt that trying to provide 'continuum parenting' in a western culture made far too many demands on western mothers who sadly do not, as tribal people do, have constant access to other willing pairs of hands to help with carrying the baby. I came to think that it may be a mistake to choose one theory from birth onwards and stick religiously to it throughout babyhood.

Statistics on parents' changing approaches as babies grow and develop (see box below) in fact show my experience to be a common one.

Where do most babies sleep?

ALSPAC 4 week figures from mothers in the Bristol area (6 month figures in brackets)

- **77.1 per cent** (33.3 per cent) of babies sleep in the mother's bedroom in their own cradle, etc.
- Although only **2.1 per cent** (2.5 per cent) are actually in the mother's bed at the start of the night, a total of **64.6 per cent** (49.8 per cent) of babies are taken into the bed when they wake at night: 14.4 per cent (7.9 per cent) always; 9.7 per cent (7.4 per cent) usually; and 40.5 per cent (34.5 per cent) sometimes.

It is clear that bed-sharing is much more common with younger babies and these figures echo those from other more recent studies. New research at the University of Durham has found that, amongst mothers from the Teeside area, a third of mothers always or often (at least twice a week) bed-shared at the 4-week stage, falling to a fifth of mothers at the 12-week stage. As with the ALSPAC study, it was only a small percentage (3.9) of families where the family bed was the baby's *only* night-time sleeping place; in the Durham study this was found to be because those families actively supported 'the family bed' philosophy.

Is bed-sharing safe?

The scientific jury is still out on the issue of whether bed-sharing, when all safety precautions are taken, just reduces or actually eliminates risk factors for SIDS. One study found no increased risk as long as the parents were not smokers – other enthusiasts quote studies apparently proving that bed-sharing protects against SIDS. However, a US paediatric association recently announced: 'There is insufficient data to conclude … that bed-sharing is clearly hazardous or clearly safe'. If you wish to adopt a policy which is 100 per cent proven to reduce your baby's SIDS risk, then as things stand you should *room*-share, rather than *bed*-share.

What the FSID recommend

The Foundation for the Study of Infant Death or FSID (see the help section) gives the following advice:

- **Room**-sharing (where the baby sleeps in a cot in your bedroom) has a positive effect in reducing the incidence of SIDS (Sudden Infant Death Syndrome or 'cot death') in the first 6 months of a baby's life.
- **Bed**-sharing poses an increased risk in certain situations. This risk may be reduced if certain safety precautions are followed. (See safety section below.)

One reason that the first 6 months is important is that after this age a baby is much more able to regulate her own breathing and temperature. If you are planning to put your newborn baby to sleep in a separate room, for safety's sake it might be worth reconsidering, at least for the early weeks.

Why do parents choose to bed-share?

A Durham University study ('Reasons to bed-share') found that the most common reason given was for ease of breast-feeding. Other research has found that mothers who bed-share tend to breast-feed for longer than those who do not. Other reasons given for bed-sharing were

- it settles a restless or ill baby;
- it reassures the mother about the baby's safety;
- it provides baby-contact time for working mothers (47 per cent of those working bed-shared);
- it is the chosen family ideology.

How long should bed-sharing continue?

If you do decide to bed-share in the early weeks, when should you stop? This is obviously a personal decision. Most people choose to have their baby established in her own sleeping place between 3–6 months of age, and this is a policy I support as the best one for ensuring your child develops independent sleeping habits. There can be disadvantages in continuing longer than this, and these are outlined below. However, if you wish to bed-share longer-term, if you are fully aware of the risks and the safety precautions, if it fits with your lifestyle and it is causing you no problems, then it is not my intention to suggest you do otherwise!

Pros and cons of short- and long-term bed-sharing

Pros – short-term bed-sharing (0–3 months)

- It promotes breast-feeding.
- Advocates of bed-sharing believe it protects against SIDS as long as certain precautions are taken – particularly non-smoking. (The jury is still 'out' on this!)
- This view is based partly upon studies showing that a parent sleeping close to a baby helps to regulate the baby's own breathing and body temperature.
- Many mothers feel more 'bonded' with their baby.

Cons – short-term bed-sharing (0–3 months)

- In certain situations it increases the risk of SIDS.
- There is also a small risk of death from accident in the bed (smothering, falling, or getting trapped in any *gaps* – such as those between a bed and the wall).

It is important to get these risks into perspective. If bed-sharing was a *major* danger, human beings would not have made it to the 21st century, as we have been doing it for quite a long time! However, it seems that more primitive sleeping places probably contained fewer hazards than modern bedrooms, and that other risk factors such as smoking and drug/alcohol intake were not so widespread.

Pros of long-term bed-sharing (6 months plus)

- You are maintaining a practice which has been historically common world-wide.
- It can be a way for parents, especially those who work in the day, to be close to their baby for long periods.
- Some families find the experience enriching and bonding.

I grew up in India. All my childhood memories are of children sleeping in their parents' bed until the next one came along and then sleeping with one or more siblings. I have adopted this policy with my own children. My partner is very happy to sleep in his own room most of the time and everyone is content.

Sue, Somerset

Cons of long-term bed-sharing

1 Effects on your child's sleep and health

- Many children who are light-sleepers sleep *less* well if bed-sharing.
- It can be harder to wean an older baby who persists in night breast-feeding after the mother wants to stop – this was also Mrs. Beeton's opinion!
- It will be harder to implement a sleep programme if required later.
- It can be harder to accustom an older child to moving out of the bed.
- Under certain conditions there can be a small extra risk of SIDS.

2 Effects on your freedom and on family relationships

- Your child may start needing you in bed with them to fall asleep – thus limiting your social life.
- If the child is asked to move out when a sibling arrives, this can cause jealousy.
- Relationships can suffer badly if both partners are not equally behind this policy.
- You may need another room in your house for intimacy with your partner.

3 Other points to consider

- Single parents *may* continue bed-sharing longer as a substitute for a partner – then wish to evict the child when a new partner arrives!
- Some experts think that bed-sharing may be psychologically inappropriate for healthy development in a western culture.

Whatever you choose, it is important to discuss and agree it with your partner. Form a policy and stick to it – it is not fair on your child to keep chopping and changing. Also, if you choose to bed-share long term, make sure you understand both your motives for and the long-term implications of this choice. There are plenty of books available which will give you positive support for this choice. If you make such a choice, embrace it happily and don't worry!

> At 12 months our baby Rory was a very light sleeper, always wanting to suck, and still breast-feeding at night. My wife was advised to take him into her bed so they could both get some sleep and I moved to the spare room. I wasn't happy with this policy but felt my wife didn't listen to anything I said. We were not spending any time together as husband/wife because as soon as Rory was quiet, she immediately needed to rest as well.
>
> *Paul McClelland, Italy*

Safety section for bed-sharing

Please read this, even if you only plan to bed-share occasionally.
You must *not* bed-share

- if you are a smoker;
- if you have been drinking;
- if you are taking any kind of drug or medication which could cause drowsiness;
- if you are excessively tired.

How to make your bed 'baby-friendly'

There are various things you can do to maximise safety if bed-sharing – I certainly followed the policy of putting my mattress on the bedroom floor to prevent the risk of falling.

- Always keep pillows well away from our baby's head.
- Make sure bedding never covers her head.
- Ensure she sleeps on her back.
- Use sheets/blankets rather than a duvet or quilt.
- A mattress on the floor (to avoid falling out) is often used.
- There must be *no* crevices anywhere – check for gaps between mattress and wall, for example.
- Generally, your baby is best off between two partners rather than between you and a wall.

In the bedroom

- Ensure no smoking (ideally none in the house at all).
- Bedroom temperature should ideally be 18°C/64°F (overheating is thought to be one cause of SIDS).

Never risk falling asleep on a sofa with your baby

One of the highest-risk practices in terms of SIDS is to fall asleep on a sofa with your baby – the risk of your baby dying is 50 times higher than with other sleep options. You should not breast-feed whilst reclining on a sofa as you could fall asleep by mistake; neither should you lie down on a sofa with your baby as a way of getting her to drop off in the evening. Sofas are NOT safe places for co-sleeping – there are too many risks for SIDS, suffocation and getting trapped.

If you only bed-share occasionally, and you have gone to sleep with your baby before your partner comes to bed, please make sure that he or she is aware that your baby is in bed with you. Then your partner can behave appropriately (for example, not sleep right next to the baby if planning to drink alcohol, or taking medication, etc.)

General safety points: baby's sleeping place

Sleeping position and clothing

- Lay baby to sleep on her back.
- Lay her with her feet at the end of her cot, with covers no higher than her shoulders, and properly tucked in.
- Remove her hat or bonnet when she is sleeping indoors.
- Never tie a dummy to your baby with string, ribbon or cord.

Sleeping environment

- No smoking in the nursery/bedroom, ideally none in the house.
- Get a nursery thermometer and maintain approx. 18°C/64°F.
- Check your baby's temperature by touching her stomach.
- Make sure that pets do not have access to the nursery.

The mattress

- Make sure it is firm and fits tightly with no gaps.
- Use a new one which is easy to keep clean and well aired (PVC cover or removable washable cover). There is a link between SIDS and secondhand mattresses.

The cot and bedding

- Make sure the cot complies with modern safety standards.
- Do not use cot pillows.
- Use sheet and baby blankets, not duvets or quilts.
- Consider using a specially designed baby sleep bag for older babies who kick off their covers (see the useful products guide).

Safe sleeping in the day

If your baby is in day-care, you are advised to make sure that your care provider understands these safety points. About a fifth of SIDS in the USA occur while babies are in day-care.

5

Preparing for a
baby sleep programme
for parents of babies aged 6 months or more

The long day's task is done, and we must sleep.
William Shakespeare   *Antony and Cleopatra*

If you are new to this guide, have not had the chance to use the preventive methods in Section 3 with your baby when he was younger, and currently have a baby over 6 months who is still waking regularly at night, you are strongly advised to use this preparatory section and the questionnaire. (It is also good to go back and read Section 3, if you have not already done so, as this may help you understand why the problem has arisen and give you some initial ideas for changes you can implement.)

Why preparation is important

- Changing your baby's routines may in itself cure any sleep problem.
- Without preparation the sleep programme (next section) may not work.
- If his night waking is due to mainly physical or emotional causes – and not just to bad habits – it may not be fair on him to start a full sleep programme.

At around this age (6 months), some important changes take place which show us that babies are now ready to enter a new phase and require (or can certainly easily adapt to) different routines from before. These changes can occur slightly earlier or later depending upon the individual baby.

'Self-soothing' habits can include: thumb-sucking, rocking, stroking something soft, or attachment to a special blanket or cuddly toy. Such habits are apparently neither a sign of anxiety, nor are they necessary for all children. However, if they become established then obviously they become part of your bedtime routine, which is fine. How you respond to night crying, *after this age particularly,* will form your baby's future sleeping habits. As has already been explained, if you have been rocking, feeding or patting/stroking him back to sleep at the slightest cry, you have actually been teaching him that he cannot go back to sleep without your help.

Changes at the 6 month stage

- Babies often begin to create new 'self-soothing' habits of their own.
- They are now sufficiently aware that you still exist when not immediately at their side – as well as that crying can have certain results.
- If you have been carrying out certain actions to get your baby to sleep it now becomes even more important to change your routines.
- Babies who have previously 'slept through' may begin to start waking up again.

Many babies who have previously slept through the night began to wake up again after 6 months. The reasons for this are not fully clear and may be varied – but the important factor here is your response to the waking.

When Emma was 5 months old she was sleeping through. Then she started waking every two hours at 6 months of age. For two weeks my husband and I took turns going in and checking on her, giving her the pacifier and covering her back up.

Angela Brewer, Spokane USA

I instituted the routines you suggested at bedtime, before I tried them during the night, and Lucas started to sleep through within a week. I never had to let him cry at all.

Jennifer Keay, Holland

> Luckily for us, within 3 days our baby Rory's sleeping has improved dramatically, providing his routine of bath, milk, sleep is always followed.
>
> *Paul McClelland, Italy*

The questionnaire below relates to important preparatory steps, which in themselves may earn you better sleep at night, and may mean you do not need to embark on the second part of the programme. If you have been using this guide during the previous weeks, you may find that much of what follows is already in place.

Are you ready for a sleep programme?

Please complete the questionnaire below, using a pencil if you think you might want to re-use this guide another time. At the end is a blank space for you to create your own action list of what you need to attend to before proceeding with Section 6.

1 **Does your baby have a regular daytime schedule of feeding and/or meals?**

From 6 months on, whether breast- or bottle-fed, or on solids, is he in general on a 3-4 hourly feeding routine, with no frequent snacks in between other than occasional drinks or short breast-feeds?

☐ YES – go to next question.

☐ NO – note down this point on the action list on page 43 and speak to your health visitor or NCT breast-feeding counsellor if you need help to get him onto such a routine.

A regular routine for feeding and mealtimes is necessary because babies try to replicate at night what they experience during the day. You should aim not to comfort-feed him, whether with breast, bottle, or other food, if he is upset during the day, as this can pave the way for night waking and possibly for eating disorders later in life.

2 Does your baby have one or more daytime sleeps at the same time every day?

☐ YES – go to next question.

☐ NO – note this on the action list. Start to regulate daytime sleeps (whether or not he initially seems tired every day) and speak to your health visitor if you need help.

A regular daytime sleep schedule is necessary because too much (or too little) daytime sleep, or sleep too late in the day, will interfere with night-time sleep. If your baby sleeps until after 3.30 in the afternoon, gradually put him down earlier *by ten minutes every day* until you have achieved the desired time. If he still sleeps for too long, you will have to wake him a little earlier every day.

3 Does your baby have a dummy or comfort bottle during the day?

☐ NO – go to next question.

☐ YES – note this on your action list, read the points below and speak to your health visitor if you still need help.

Bottles of milk or juice at night are a very bad habit and can contribute to middle-ear problems and tooth decay. A dummy may fall out of his mouth at night and he will need you to replace it. Use of a dummy at night has a protective effect against SIDS but *can* make a sleep programme more difficult. Either wean him off it by first decreasing his amount of *daytime* use through offering extra attention and diversions – or consider putting two or three in the cot to increase the chances of him finding one at night! (Weaning him off it may initially cause crying but he will learn new routines. Thumb sucking is better for a sleep programme in this respect.)

4 Is your baby out of your bed and in a separate cot (preferably in a different room)?

☐ YES – go to next question.

☐ NO – note this on the action list and re-read Section 4.

Whilst it is entirely your choice where your baby sleeps, experience shows that it can be harder to resolve night-waking when he is still in your bed – particularly if you also need to wean him. You may also find it harder to carry out the sleep programme with him in your room in a separate cot. If you do not have a separate bedroom available for your baby, consider making a temporary arrangement during the programme period so that he can have his own room while he learns better sleeping habits, but give him a few days to get used to the room before starting the programme.

5 Is your baby still feeding during the night, and waking up less than 9 hours after his bedtime feed?

☐ YES – note this on the action list and turn to Appendix 1

☐ NO – go to next question

If he is breast-feeding during the night then he may well have developed an association between needing to suck and falling back to sleep, particularly if you usually 'feed him to sleep' at bedtime. If your baby sucks *for a minute or less* upon waking, or if you do not feel that he is taking in much milk, then he is not really dependent on the food, only on the breast. In this case, you can wean him off the breast as part of the sleep programme. If, however, your baby is taking in large amounts of milk at night (whether from breast or bottle), or significant amounts of other drinks (e.g. juice) then it is important to begin weaning him off this before commencing the programme – read Appendix 1 to get help with this.

6 Is your baby physically well?

☐ YES – double check the list below, then go to next question.

☐ NO – consult with your doctor if he is listless, seems unwell or has any of the following symptoms:
  • excessive crying
  • loud snoring (which can mean breathing difficulties)
  • rubbing the ears, or red ears (which can mean middle-ear infection)
  • pulling the knees up to the chest (which can mean colic or digestive difficulties)
  • a lack of wet nappies (which could be urinary tract infection)
  • a rash anywhere on the body
or if there are any other physical symptoms that worry you. Teething pain, nappy rash/discomfort, food allergy, nasal congestion, colds/flu or sore throat can also obviously interfere with sleep.

Do not commence a sleep programme until the baby is physically well. If you are at all nervous about commencing the sleep programme, seek reassurance from your doctor or health visitor first. See also the medical note on page 42.

7 Is it possible that your baby is suffering from a food allergy?

Does he suffer from one or more of the symptoms below?
- Eczema or any allergies
- Frequent ear or chest infections (with or without frequent antibiotic use)
- Excessive restlessness or crying (extreme 'colic')
- Dribbling or excessive head banging or cot rocking
- Persistent diarrhoea
- Regular vomiting
- Previous exceptional activity whilst in the womb
- Abnormal thirst during the day or at night[1] and/or poor appetite.
- Or does the baby's mother suffer from any of the following: migraine, hay fever, rhinitis, arthritis, food allergy/sensitivity, asthma or eczema?

☐ NO – go to next question.

☐ YES – this increases the possibility of food allergy or sensitivity. Add to your action list and read Appendix 4. Then speak to your doctor or ideally a qualified nutritional therapist as soon as possible (see the help section). It is possible that poor sleep is connected to diet.

8 Is there a bad emotional atmosphere in the house?

Are there really bad tensions *which have been going on for some time*, apart from the possible recent stress caused by sleep deprivation?

☐ NO – go to next question.

☐ YES – note on the action list and contact Relate (details in the help section) – or consult your doctor about whether there is counselling available on the NHS in your area. If you have been feeling continually weepy, depressed or hopeless since the birth, please pluck up the courage to talk to your health visitor about whether you might be affected by post-natal depression (also see the help section for PND helplines).

---

1   This can also be caused by feeding him a salty diet – some adult foods contain a lot more sodium than is ideal for a baby. Watch crisps and processed foods (burgers, sausages, etc.).

Do seek help, as strained relationships and bad atmospheres in the house will almost certainly affect your baby, cause extra distress and probably affect sleep. If the stress is actually caused by lack of sleep, then it is urgent that you seek support to ensure the successful outcome of a sleep programme as soon as possible.

9 Do you feel a strong attachment and bond of love with your baby?

In your opinion, is he put down to sleep feeling as loved and secure as possible?

☐ YES – go to next question.

☐ NO – note on the action list and speak to your health visitor.

Sometimes, through no fault of the parents (as in very premature births, other birth complications or post-natal depression), normal bonding does not take place and a mother can feel a lack of love for her child. If this happens, or if the person the baby is most attached to is regularly absent at bedtime, then the baby's crying at night may be caused by distress about this. However, lack of sleep can also affect the mother's feelings about the baby from the start, so it is important that you seek specialist professional guidance a.s.a.p. to develop a plan of action (see page 65).

10 Does your baby (at ten months and over) experience *intense* separation anxiety during the day?

Does he react to daytime separation with *severe* panic and fear (not just a small amount of crying which can be easily comforted once you have gone)?

☐ NO – go to next question.

☐ YES – note on the action list. You may have to wean him off you more gradually at night, using the graded approach – see Appendix 3.

11 Is one cause of waking that your baby kicks off his bedding at night and then gets cold?

☐ NO – go to next question.

☐ YES – note on the action list and see the useful products guide.

Babies are less able to regulate their body temperature than adults, so to be both safe and comfortable you should use a nursery thermometer to check the temperature and use appropriate background heating in cold weather. In order to guard against night waking due to covers being kicked loose or to safeguard against covers kicked over the head, parents in many continental countries use a low-tog baby sleeping-bag or 'kicking bag' from 4 months, which I have personally found to be excellent.

12 **Are you willing to let your baby cry for short periods at night if necessary during the next stage of the sleep programme?**

☐ YES

☐ NO – note on the action list and turn to Appendix 2. You can also get reassurance from your doctor or health visitor about this aspect. If you really cannot tolerate this, you may have to use the alternative graded approach (Appendix 3). But even this approach involves small amounts of crying and does take much longer to achieve results.

Medical note

If your baby suffers from asthma or bad eczema or is currently suffering from an infectious (or any other) illness, then you must not carry out the programme in the next section before seeking medical advice.

- The asthmatic child may need the amended technique in Appendix 3.
- A child with eczema may need extra medication to reduce itching. Eczema can also be treated with infant food and EFA supplements; see the practitioner list for how to get individual or telephone nutritional advice.

If your problems are extremely severe, or if your child has a neurological disorder, learning disability or other handicap, these techniques are probably suitable and will be effective, but you should also seek medical advice before proceeding. If your baby was premature but is otherwise well, delay the start of the programme by the length of his prematurity. If she is over 18 months of age please read one of the recommended books in the reading list for older children, before commencing. However, previously ill or premature babies, once fully recovered and/ or developing normally, can still benefit from this programme.

Your Preparatory Action List

I/we need to take action about the following things:

. . . .

. . . .

. . . .

. . . .

. . . .

. . . .

. . . .

. . . .

. . . .

. . . .

. . . .

. . . .

. . . .

. . . .

. . . .

This list is what you need to address *before* commencing the sleep programme. If these lines are blank then you are ready to begin the programme. If you have only one or two preparatory changes to make you may deal with this section rapidly. Others may have to change several aspects of their own and their baby's behaviour before beginning the programme itself. Don't be put off if you encounter some temporary extra crying while he breaks these habits. Even if you think you will be willing to let him discharge this distress by crying, do read Appendix 2 as this can strengthen your resolve; and try to discuss this with your health visitor, who will help you plan which items to deal with first.

6

The baby sleep programme

for babies 6 months and over

Close thine eyes and sleep secure;
Thy soul is safe, thy body sure.
Charles I

Key features of a 'baby sleep programme'

- You change your baby's immediate environment and your own behaviour towards her.
- You give your baby the opportunity to learn to put herself to sleep.
- It is a safe, proven and highly effective approach which will be successful in the vast majority – some experts say 90 per cent – of cases, usually within just a few days.

Jack, eight months, has gone from waking every two hours in the night to having 11 hours unbroken sleep at night, as well as sleeping up to 2 hours during the day. What a relief – he is happy and smiling on waking, well-rested and with energy for the rest of the day.

Maree White, Bath.

Twelve steps to perfect sleep

Congratulations! You have decided to take action. The most important thing now is a positive attitude and to believe in your ability to take control of the situation. You may have become demoralised, exhausted and convinced the situation will never change. Take a deep breath. These techniques do work, they are medically approved and used by experts. (**But see medical note at the end of Section 5 before embarking on this programme.**) You will not harm your baby and in a few days you will be more rested and in a much better state to look after her, and other children if you have them.

Be determined to do it, know it will work, and this will make it far more likely to. Remember, you can be firm and loving at the same time. You must believe that you and your baby have developed a bad habit, that she needs your help in breaking it, and that you would be letting her down to give in and not follow the programme.

When to start the programme

Although you can start this programme at any time from 6 months onwards, I recommend starting *before* the natural 'separation anxiety' stage which begins between nine to ten months of age and which lasts up to a month. During this time babies become more aware of themselves as separate from their mother (or main carer), may cry more for her or him during the day and *may* therefore be more likely to cry at night during their natural night waking. You should not, however, let this discourage you from embarking upon the programme at this stage, just realise that results may be *slightly* less consistent during this particular short period.

It may be worth delaying the programme slightly if your baby
- has been recently unsettled by a big change (house move, you returning to work, etc.);
- is ill or teething particularly badly;
- is crying and feeding a lot more than usual – this could be a 'growth spurt' (see page 25).

Does my baby have to cry during the programme?

Whenever we have to change or break a habit we feel distress. Adults do not always cry when they feel distress since they have learned to 'control their feelings'. But babies are programmed to cry at the slightest distress and, by 6+ months, your baby may have inadvertently been 'trained' by you that she has to cry to get what she (currently) needs in order to get to sleep again. Having developed bad habits, babies will not want to change – it is easier for them to maintain the status quo. So initially they may cry. If you try to stop your baby crying then change will be more difficult. However, this book does not recommend letting babies cry for extended periods without reassurance and checking, which will make things less distressing for you and easier for your baby.

> Real proof that letting babies cry is *not* cruel comes from talking to the parents of infants who have been through a sleep programme, whose children wake up happy and full of beans in the morning, after considerable crying the night before, and smile happily up at them from their cot. Read Appendix 2 if you are unsure or worried about this.

If bad habits have already become established, the change of routine usually causes some complaint to begin with, but the 'Quick Check Method' – where you go in regularly to reassure and check your baby – will keep any crying at a minimum level and one which is acceptable to you.

> Above all, Freya remained cheerful in the daytime throughout the procedure, and seems to benefit greatly from her new-found ability to get a good night's sleep.
>
> *Ian and Margaret Rock, Cumbria*

Your Parental Questionnaire and Agreement

This section is for parents who have made the changes on their action list and whose baby is still needing their help to get to sleep at night, and/or is waking frequently at night and needing help to get back to sleep. The preparatory action list was so that you could rule out any possibility that your baby is waking at night for reasons connected with lack of routine, physical illness/allergy or emotional upset, rather than because she has got into bad habits. Having done that, what now needs to be done is to help her change those habits and learn how to put herself to sleep.

I have designed this as an agreement, because formal agreements can help strengthen our resolve. (Omit Section 10 if following the graded approach in Appendix 3.)

> *Note for single parents* I have used 'we' throughout, even though I am aware that many people will be facing this task on their own. Perhaps try to get help from a supportive friend/relative, as this will make it much easier to carry out the programme.

1 Have we carried out all the preparatory changes as far as we feel able?

☐ YES – continue.

☐ NO – if you feel unable to make all these changes without help, contact your health visitor before continuing with this agreement.

2 We will make the following changes to our baby's room/immediate surroundings/bedding before we start the programme:

. . . .

. . . .

. . . .

. . . .

. . . .

. . . .

Things to consider are: putting a dim nightlight into the room so that your baby can see her surroundings on waking and will be less likely to feel afraid; getting a nursery thermometer to make sure the room is not too hot or cold; getting a blind at the window to cut out early morning light in the summer months; cutting down background noise in the baby's room; and removing from the room objects you may need to get during sleep hours so that you do not have to disturb her. If the cot is in a position near a door or passageway you may also consider moving it to ensure the least disturbance.

3 **Are we willing to make a commitment to follow the programme consistently, for at least seven consecutive nights?**

☐ YES – continue.

☐ NO – *Note: It would not be fair to the child to begin it and then stop suddenly, and the programme would clearly not be successful.*

4 **Choosing our date – We will follow the programme described below for at least seven consecutive nights from .... (day) .... (date) to .... (day) .... (date) inclusive and have written these dates on our calendar/diary.**

Find 7 nights when you can afford to be tired the next day (for at least the first 3 days) if necessary – perhaps a weekend/time off, etc. If neighbours can hear sound from your house, you should consult with/inform them or wait until they are away. (If they refuse to allow any noise in the night you will have to use the alternative method in Appendix 3, or even go away to a relative's house during the programme period.) Results are often gained after only 3 nights, but making a commitment to 7 days will give you enough time to see good progress.

5 **From .... (date) we are *not* going to do the following to help our baby go to sleep at night, or during the day:**

Write down the actions you usually engage in to get your baby to sleep in the day or night-time, e.g.: breast-feeding, stroking, rocking, sitting with baby etc. Note: You can use these as part of the bedtime routine, but not actually as the child is dropping off to sleep.

. . . .

. . . .

. . . .

6 Who can help us?

Make a list: friends, relatives or baby-sitters you will contact to ask for daytime help during the first three days. Why not make the phone calls NOW? (This is less essential for those using the alternative graded approach.)

. . . .

. . . .

. . . .

It may only take half an hour to get your baby to sleep the first night, but it is possible you could be up for several hours for the first night. Get help in order to preserve your baby's routine during the day, or to allow you to have an afternoon nap.

7 The new bedtime routine will begin at . . . . pm and the new bedtime will be . . . . pm (approx. 30–60 minutes later). The last feed will be at . . . . pm (ideally at least 15 minutes before bedtime).

Choose a time when your baby usually appears tired and which suits your life – usually between 6 and 8 p.m., depending on when you wish your baby to wake up (unless she has been going to bed extremely late, in which case choose a compromise time and gradually move the bedtime earlier once this programme has been carried out). Keep this time as peaceful and happy as possible. Initially, the adult she is most attached to (usually the mother) should be present every night. Later, other adults (father, babysitter, granny etc.) can take over so that the routine, rather than the mother's presence, becomes the key to sleep. Once the time is chosen, stick to it.

8 This will be the bedtime routine:

1   . . . .

2   . . . .

3   . . . .

4   The routine will end with . . . .

This can include quiet games, stories, bath-time, lullabies, baby massage. Use your rocking, swinging, patting, etc. during this time, but not when you put your baby down. The sequence of events should be the same every night, predictable *and with a clear ending point.* If you are giving a new security object (see next point), introduce it now.

9 **We will give our baby** . . . . **for comfort and security.**

Giving a 'transitional object' (such as a teddy, favourite sheet/blanket, etc.) may help to give your child a feeling of reassurance and control. Your baby may already have one, or you can use this time to give a new teddy or other toy. Choose a security object which does not need you to adjust it in the night. If your baby was previously using a dummy you may perhaps have already replaced this with something else.

10 **Once our baby is in bed, we are willing to allow crying for** . . . .
  (number between 1 to 5 – ideally 5) minutes, before going in.

The checking routine will be explained on page 53.

Initially, aim for as near to five minutes crying as you can bear. If, after reading Appendix 2 and discussing it with your health visitor, you are really unable to face allowing your baby to cry for short periods, then use the amended technique in Appendix 3 and do not complete the above section.

11 . . . . **(name of parent) will do the bedtime checks/graded**
  leaving – (*graded leaving is for the alternative technique in Appendix 3*) –
  and agrees not to pick our baby up unless physical safety demands it (e.g.
  in the case of vomiting). If she wakes before . . . . **am (your target**
  early morning feed time, 9+ hours from the bedtime feed) we will follow
  the same crying/checking routine.

Follow the additional instructions on page 73 if completing the night weaning. If she was previously having several feeds at night you may initially need to eliminate the first one or two and then gradually work on the remaining early morning feeds. If you are following the alternative method, write here the name of the parent who will put the baby to bed and carry out the graded leaving approach each bedtime.

12 . . . . **(name of parent/helper) will do the checks (+ graded**
  leaving if following alternative approach) from. . . . . **pm to** . .
  . . . . **pm/am; and** . . . . **(name of other parent/**
  helper) will do from . . . . **am to** . . . . **am.**

Splitting the night into shifts initially will help with sleep deprivation.

We have completed all the above sections and agree to follow the baby sleep programme.

Signed .... Date ....

and .... other parent (or helper if applicable)

In particular, I found the contract an excellent idea. It strengthened my resolve to carry on.

Natasha Radford, Essex

Getting support

Before starting the programme, to give yourself the best chance of success, you are strongly advised to enlist the support of your health visitor, family, friends, neighbours, and most importantly, your partner. If there is a local sleep clinic, do try to attend it.

- **Your health visitor**   Show her your plan of action. Whether or not she runs a group, just having her on the end of the phone as a support during the programme will give you enormous moral support.
- **Your local sleep clinic**   These are usually run by health visitors who help parents either individually or by running a group sleep programme. (Telephone the Karvol Sleep Management Service if you wish to find out where your nearest one is, see page 65.)
- **Your doctor**   You need to speak to him/her if you are really concerned about your baby's health or about any possible risks to it from this programme.
- **Your family, friends and neighbours**   Tell everyone that you are going to do it, for this will make it harder to back out of! Others' criticism during the programme period is particularly damaging – you need to prevent this in advance by satisfying any doubts of anxious mothers-in-law, etc.

- **Your partner**   Get him/her to read this book. Your partner's support is particularly important. Make a time to sit down and complete the parental agreement together (below), if your child still needs further help after you have made the above changes.

Starting your own sleep clinic

If you really feel you need the support of a group to make the changes, you can start your own. One way is by advertising locally for other parents and then inviting a local psychologist, social worker or health visitor to come along. The Karvol Sleep Management Service provides free advice to health visitors on how to start a group. However, if you do not have a support group, do not let this put you off. Unless your child falls into the categories on page 42, you should be able to deal with the problem using the self-help methods in this guide.

Putting it into action

Day one onwards

Read this section once to prepare for day one of the programme and again on the first day itself. It is designed to act as a step-by-step guide to complement the agreement and to answer any questions that may arise. I am assuming that you have carried out all the necessary preparations in the agreement (such as changes to the baby's room and organising help for the next few days if possible).

If you are following the amended technique in Appendix 3, omit points marked with * and read this in conjunction with the Graded Leaving method instructions.

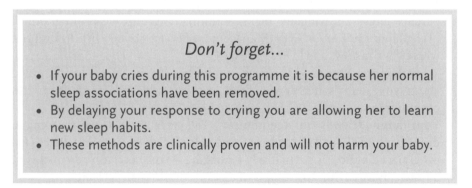

Don't forget...

- If your baby cries during this programme it is because her normal sleep associations have been removed.
- By delaying your response to crying you are allowing her to learn new sleep habits.
- These methods are clinically proven and will not harm your baby.

Day One

Put your baby to bed

Before bed, carry out the bedtime routine as planned in Point 7 on page 49 number]. Keep everything calm and happy – act calm, even if you do not feel it!

- Take your baby to her cot/bed.
- Feed in the nursery if necessary (but do not allow your baby to go to sleep during the feed).
- Dim the lighting, put your baby into the bed/cot, tuck her up, make sure the comfort object is present if needed, say: *Go to sleep* firmly and calmly.
- Check the nursery thermometer and temperature of room, check that the nightlight is on if you wish to have one, and that you have everything you need from the room.
- * Leave the room while the child is still awake, even if she cries for you.

Make sure that the room is the same when you leave it as it will be in the middle of the night – i.e. no music playing, extra lights on, etc.

Complete the Sleep Diary

Turn to the sleep diary at the end of this guide – and begin to complete it as per the instructions. Try not to get too stressed about any crying which you hear (see Appendix 2 for methods of dealing with your stress about this). Whoever is doing the checking should time the crying with a watch – it can seem far longer than it really is. If you are following the graded approach, you should complete the diary afterwards.

Carry out the Checking Procedure (not for graded approach)

* **First check**   Leave your baby alone for the agreed period of time (between 1-5 minutes – ideally 5) even if she is crying. Then, unless it seems that the crying is dying down, whoever has agreed to do the first check goes calmly and confidently into the baby's room. Tuck her up if she has got out of the blankets, give back the comfort object if necessary – but do not pick your baby up or engage in previous rituals; say: *Go to sleep,* and leave the room again, even if she is still crying or sounding furious.

* **Second check**   Leave your baby alone for double the length of time in 4 above   (2 minutes minimum, ideally 10 minutes). Repeat the procedure in 4, above. *Remember, if crying sounds as if it is dying down, do not go back in but wait until it dies down.*

* **Third check**   Leave your baby alone for 15 minutes max (If you began with 3 or less minutes, keep doubling the time until you reach 15). Subsequent checks should be every 15 minutes. Keep completing the diary.

* Many people will only need to do three checks at the first bedtime. A typical first night's response can be 1-2 hours' crying. However, for entrenched problems you will need to continue this for several hours. If it looks like continuing, you might need to take it in turns to go to sleep (with earplugs if necessary) – or at least try to watch TV!

Get some sleep yourself!

You will probably wish to go to sleep yourselves to build up energy for any possible waking during the night. Take a clock (so you will know what time it is if she wakes) and the sleep chart with you. Couples may find it more practical, if they have the space, to sleep separately during the programme period, in order to minimise sleep deprivation.

How to deal with night waking

Remember – babies do wake naturally at night; but if they cry you have already decided which parent will deal with this at which time of night. Never go in straight away, even if following the graded approach. Follow the same checking routine exactly, and keep completing the sleep chart. If you are too exhausted to cope, wake the other parent and ask them to continue with the process. *(See Appendix 3 for graded approach to checking.)*

On no account give in

Having started the programme you would now strengthen your baby's belief that crying works and make it harder to begin again. Consistency is the key.

Day Two

The next morning

Even if you and your baby are exhausted from the first night, you must wake her as near as possible to the normal time and follow the daytime routine, otherwise your baby's sleep/wake cycle will shift and make the programme harder to follow.

Daytime sleeps on day two

Again, follow the same routine, put her down awake and either leave or follow the graded approach. Do quick checks at the same intervals if she cries. Keep completing the diary.

Try to get some rest yourself during the day. Hopefully you will have arranged some help – perhaps someone can look after your baby for you so that you can have a nap yourself if you need one.

* **At bedtime** follow the same procedures as the previous night, but you can build the checking intervals to 20 minutes.

Results are often much improved on the second night. In the case of my first child, crying time dropped from 27 minutes on day one to 10 minutes on day two (3 minutes on day three, none on day four...). Results may be slower with the alternative graded approach.

Day Three

Repeat the procedure for Day Two. Results are almost always significantly better, but don't give up if there is still some crying. You will be able to see any progress clearly on your sleep chart. Even if you are one of the cases where the whole process takes a week or more (longer with the graded approach), this is still a small price to pay for the improvements your family will eventually experience.

Day Four and beyond

By now you should begin to see light at the end of the tunnel. If not, then use the next section to check whether you are making any mistakes.

Night one   We put Boris to sleep in the usual way, and he woke up at about 1 am. It took me about 1½ hours to get him to sleep again. He didn't wake up again that night.

Night two   I put him to sleep following the agreed routine again. He took 20 minutes to fall asleep. He didn't wake up at all that night.

Night three   I put him to sleep in the same way and he took 3 minutes to fall asleep. He has slept through the night ever since.

Dejan and Ana Deletic, Aberdeen

Everyone is gaining weight, we're eating properly, we have a social life – our little angel is blooming and we now have the energy to enjoy our son.

Sharon Birmingham, Somerset

7
Results and frequently asked questions

Oh, why did I awake?
When shall I sleep again?
Housman *A Shropshire Lad*

In general you should see a significant reduction in your baby's crying time after three nights and, if not a full cure, then certainly a full night's sleep after a week (with slower progress likely using the alternative graded approach). If he was previously feeding very frequently during the night, it may take slightly longer, but even in this case you will see progress after a week, which will encourage you to keep going.

What to do if things don't work

If you have put all of the above into operation and you are not seeing progress, certainly after two weeks, then ask yourself the following questions:

1 **Have we fully addressed all the preparatory issues in Section 5?**

Go through Section 5 again and double check that everything was properly in place before you started the programme. It is particularly important that you re-consider the following key issues:

- **Stress**   deal with any underlying emotional problems in your family.
- **Crying**   let your child release tension by crying during the day if he really needs to (re-read Appendix 2).
- **Diet**   re-read Appendix 4 about any possible link between sleeplessness and diet/allergy – (do consider changing your own diet if breastfeeding and/or

your baby's formula or diet, even as an experiment, as it often surprises parents quite how much a child's behaviour can be affected by their diet).

2 Do we have the right attitude?

Some experts believe that your attitude (feeling and showing too much concern, or being upset yourself) can be a message to the baby that you will eventually give in, which keeps him awake and crying out for you. (Your child may also be upset that you are upset.) Your attitude – even if you find it difficult – needs to be consistently firm, calm and confident. Express your distress to your partner, not to your child.

3 Did we follow the programme every single night?

If you skip a night during the programme period, your baby may have become confused about what is going on. The confusion created is really not fair on your child. *Start again and follow the programme consistently for at least 7 days if you have skipped nights during the programme.*

4 Were we logical and consistent?

Some people still rock their babies to sleep at the beginning of the night and then let them cry for half an hour in the middle before returning to rock them again. This will not allow infants to learn the new sleep associations, so will not work. *Follow an identical approach on every night of the programme.*

If any of the above applies to you, and if you are satisfied that there are no other medical factors involved, then you could well start the programme again after a few days' break, this time making sure that you are consistent and have dealt with all the preparatory issues first. If the answer to all the above questions is YES, then ask yourself –

5 Have we really bonded with our baby?

Have you dealt with any underlying emotional problems in your family and particularly with any lack of a strong emotional love-bond with your baby, not caused directly by lack of sleep? *If he does not feel loved and for some reason you have not been able to develop the right attachment to your child, then, according to child psychologists, this could cause babies to cry at night.* A sleep programme in this case may still be important but may only be successful when you are also dealing with the underlying issues. Seek specialist help as soon as possible. If you are the main carer and you have recently returned to work, make sure you have read Appendix 5.

6 Should we alter our baby's sleeping environment?

There are products listed at the back of this book which can help ensure a more comfortable night for him (low-tog baby sleep bags and organic natural fibre mattresses, etc.). However, there is a lesser known dimension to the importance of the sleeping environment which needs to be addressed in a minority of situations – and which could provide the answer to a very unsettled baby if all other options have been eliminated. Modern homes contain a growing number of electrical appliances and circuitry which emit invisible electromagnetic fields. Although most of these are well below the levels permitted by the National Radiological Protection Board, other experts believe that constant exposure to even low-level fields, especially during sleep, can have a negative effect upon health, behaviour and sleep. These fields can be amplified by many factors – one of which is metal – another of which is naturally occurring earth radiation. If your baby sleeps in a cot with a metal sprung mattress, a cot which contains metal or has a metal base, you would be advised to change this for a wooden cot with a wooden slatted base. (In my opinion, you should do this anyway, but it is particularly important if he has sleeping problems.) In addition, if you have any electrical appliances, including breathing monitors, heaters (including radiators) and other gadgetry switched on and immediately near to the baby's head at night, you should move these (or the baby) at least three feet away from them. (The term for professionals who measure all forms of radiation is 'radiesthesist'. The address of a highly recommended practitioner can be found in the Practitioner List).

Finally, if the sleep programme fails, for whatever reason: you may need specialist help. There may be a medical or food allergy factor that has been overlooked. There are *very rare* cases of children needing only 5 or 6 hours of sleep per night. It is conceivable that you have been unsuccessful for this or some other reason (see page 65 for getting specialist help).

> The importance of a calm but firm attitude in dealing with night waking cannot be overestimated. I had never phased out our baby Anna's night-time feed, and we ended up with a 2 year old crying at the end of our bed every night at 3 am. Initially, we let her into our bed in order to get some sleep, but eventually she started throwing tantrums in the night. My husband and I were exhausted and almost hysterical. When we attended a local sleep clinic we were helped to develop a firm but calm attitude, in order to help Anna realise she had to go back to bed and stay there. Now she quite often tucks herself up.
>
> *Jill, Wiltshire*

Frequently asked questions

Isn't it cruel to let a baby cry?

I have mentioned the importance of only carrying out a baby sleep programme if (a) your baby is 6 months or over, (b) you are sure that you have dealt with all the preparatory issues in Section 5, and (c) that you also have a normal bond of love with him. See Appendix 2 on Understanding and Coping with Crying, which fully answers this question.

Might my baby not be in pain, or sick?

Pain cries are different from other cries. There is a sudden onset of loud crying (as opposed to the gradual building of other cries), a long cry at the beginning, followed by a holding of breath and then high-pitched crying. If the baby has somehow hurt himself in the cot, you will immediately know it. Sick cries are a continuous fussy, whiny, nasal cry at a low intensity. Both of these sound different to the cry you will have heard every night when he wakes and needs you to put him back to sleep. Dr. Ferber points out that if a baby wakes but then goes straight back to sleep when offered rocking or other comfort, he is obviously not in pain or sick.

Should we use drugs to help our baby sleep?

Unless drugs are required to sort out an underlying medical disorder, the consensus view on this point is that, except in very extreme cases, using drugs gives only short-term help. They will probably cause more problems in the long-term than they solve. There might conceivably be a situation where drugs could be useful for short-term crisis intervention to give parents some respite prior to a sleep programme. Unfortunately, antihistamines and sedatives are frequently prescribed, but leading sleep expert Dr. Ferber has observed an increase in daytime problem behaviour when drugs are used, as well as hyperactivity. Sedatives can also be addictive. Some antibiotics can temporarily disrupt sleep patterns and you should not carry out a sleep programme while your child is suffering from an infectious illness or taking antibiotics.

Perhaps my child only needs 6 hours sleep?

As already mentioned, this is just possible but *extremely* rare. If your child is currently only sleeping six hours each night, you should be able to extend this length using the techniques explained. Reduce or eliminate daytime naps if necessary for babies over one year in order to increase night-time sleep.

Can either the breast-feeding mother's or baby's diet affect a baby's sleep?

Yes, both are possible. Please see Appendix 4 for further information on the subject of your baby's diet. If breast-feeding, in general you should avoid

- stimulants including coca-cola, tea, coffee or chocolate;
- gas-forming foods such as sprouts, broccoli, cauliflower, onions, beans, cucumber and peppers;
- citrus fruits.

If your baby is particularly unsettled, is having sleep problems, and/or has any of the symptoms on page 40 a breast-feeding mother should avoid in addition:

- cow's-milk products (including milk, butter, yoghurt, cheese. Substitute with soya milk and yoghurts, and margarine without whey).

The advice to avoid all cow's milk products may seem extreme, but if you try it for a week and notice a definite effect, the inconvenience will be worth it.

All the above can have an effect on the baby via your milk.

On the positive side, fennel herbal tea can assist milk supply and reduce colic in the baby. Watch processed (salty) food in your baby's diet – these may cause a natural thirst which leads to crying for drinks at night.

What if my baby's crying leads to vomiting?

Vomiting is generally more common in young children than in adults, due to differences of physiology. There are a few cases where babies (usually over 15 months or so) may vomit as a reaction to a sleep programme. If this happens more than once or twice you should consider switching to the more gradual approach described in Appendix 3.

Can birth complications cause sleep problems later?

There are studies showing that babies born by Caesarian section or who suffered distress during the birth, or babies whose mothers experienced toxaemia or heavy sedation during delivery, are more likely to be wakeful than other babies. There is some evidence that Cranial Osteopathy can be useful in these cases. To find your nearest practitioner, see contact details in the Practitioner List at the end of this guide.

What if my child tries to get out of the cot?

It is obviously easier to complete a sleep programme before moving your child into his first bed. However, children who can get out of the cot must be moved into beds for safety reasons. Richard Ferber's book (see further reading section) gives excellent advice on many aspects of how to help older children with sleep problems, including advice on various strategies for encouraging children to stay in their own bedrooms. If your child is not ready to go into a bed but you are slightly worried about safety, then put cushions and pillows on the floor around the cot.

Can I use these methods for older children?

Yes, the methods are the same, but there may be extra information you need to know first, and I recommend Richard Ferber's book for this.

My child needs help to go to sleep but then sleeps through the night – so is there a problem?

No, not unless the pre-sleep ritual takes too long for you or limits your social life in a way that becomes a problem.

My baby's sleep patterns have regressed after an illness

This can also happen after a holiday or any change. Just start again, but make sure that the child has absolutely recovered from any illness, even a cold, and not taking any medication. If the techniques have already been successful once, it should be possible to re-establish the same pattern again quite quickly.

My child goes to sleep well but wakes at 5 am

If you have just begun a sleep programme with a baby who has only just given up a night feed and has managed to make it through until five am from, say, seven or eight pm, then this is excellent because he has slept nine or ten hours and may well be very hungry. In this case, feed the baby in the nursery and put him back into the cot again *awake* for another phase of sleep (following the same principles if he remains awake). Do not become a five am martyr only to put him down for a long morning sleep two or three hours later. It is much better to help him gradually learn how to sleep for the eleven- or twelve-hour period that he should be capable of.

Gradually extend the time of the morning feed by five or ten minutes every day until you have gained an extra hour over the following week or two. You are likely to find that you wake up one morning and find the clock says seven am – and your baby is still asleep! If all else fails, you can consider making bedtime an hour later, but don't expect this to work instantaneously, as your baby is likely to wake up at the normal time even if he went to bed later. For this to work, you usually have to make the entire daily schedule – naps, meals and all – an hour later too.

For determined early wakers, some health visitors recommend leaving toys in the cot for baby to play with until you are ready to start the day.

Would it help my baby to sleep if I put him onto solids?

Some people are convinced that putting a baby onto solids will help establish sleep patterns, but in my experience this only helps if the baby was not sleeping properly because he was ready for solids and not getting them. Many babies can be perfectly well-nourished on breast milk until 5 or even 6 months of age. Others need solids earlier – get your health visitor's advice. If your baby is proving to be particularly difficult to wean off night feeds then it may be that he is not getting enough nourishment in the day and is perhaps ready for solids. However, forcing babies onto solids too early may be bad for their immature digestive systems – and please do avoid feeding babies large amounts of cow's dairy products (such as yoghurts and fromage frais). My babies did not go onto solids until they were 5 months old, and I noticed no change in their sleep patterns as a result.

However, once they are on solids, some people, including myself, have found that a 'slow-release' food like oats or other whole-grain cereal, if included in the final meal of the day, will help to sustain the baby through the night better than other foods.

Further help and reading

Baby sleep consultancies in the UK

A national database of sleep clinics

Compiled by Karvol (the nasal decongestant makers). Parents and health visitors can telephone **Karvol Sleep Management Helpline** on (+44) (0)207 413 3712.

From this helpline: parents can obtain details of the nearest health visitor-run sleep clinic in their area; health visitors can ask to be sent a free pack of Karvol's sleep clinic resource materials, the magazine *Sleep Talk* – plus guidance and materials for setting up a new clinic.

Private health visitor sleep consultancy in the UK

Gill Brown (+44) (0)1491 825664, Wallingford, Oxon. (This is a fee-paying service).

Please do write in with details of any new private services run by qualified health visitors.

Getting specialist help in the UK via the NHS

If you feel you need more help than your doctor or health visitor can offer, then you can ask to be referred to your local department of child psychology or to a paediatrician, who may in turn be able to refer you to one of the very few specialist hospital sleep clinics. Sadly, the only ones in the UK at the time of writing are at Southampton General Hospital and the Park Hospital for Children in Oxford.

Further reading

Establishing routines/settling very young babies

Pantley, Elizabeth: *The No-Cry Sleep Solution*, Contemporary Books, 2002 (US/ $14.95). A gentle approach for encouraging young babies into good sleep routines. Recommended if you are determined to avoid crying at all costs – but the methods could be very time consuming!

Ford, Gina: *The Contented Little Baby Book,* Vermillion, 1999 (£7.99). For those who need help with routines: very sound, detailed 'no-nonsense' approach to establishing feeding/sleeping. Good advice on how to set up and equip your nursery.

Karp, Harvey: *The Happiest Baby,* Michael Joseph/Penguin, 2002 (£9.99). Excellent on soothing techniques for babies from 0–3 months and dealing with colic – by mimicking the womb environment (swaddling, sounds, movement, touch, etc.).

Sleep problems in older children

Ferber, R: *Solve Your Child's Sleep Problems.* Dorling Kindersley, 1st pub. 1986, (£7.99). This classic book is by a leading US expert on sleep disorders. The book gives detailed advice on topics concerning sleep problems in older children (night terrors, bed-wetting, etc.)

Quine, Lyn: *Solving Children's Sleep Problems,* Beckett Karlson, 1997 (£12.99) Amazingly detailed book, full of charts, tests, and alternative step-by-step approaches for children of all ages from birth to teenage.

Bed-sharing and early closeness

Jackson, D: *Three in a Bed.* Bloomsbury Press, 1999, 1st pub. 1989 (£12.99)

Liedloff, J: *The Continuum Concept.* Penguin Arkana, 1989, 1st pub. 1975 (£7.99)

Both these books strongly advocate bed-sharing and keeping your baby close to you in the early months. The Continuum Concept is a classic and compares Western childcare approaches with those of South American Indian people.

Coping with crying

Jackins, HJ: *The Human Side of Human Beings.* Rational Island Publishers, PO Box 2081, Main Office Station, Seattle, WA 98111, USA, 1965

Solter, AJ: *The Aware Baby.* Shining Star Press, PO Box 206, Goleta, CA 93116, 1984

See also *website*   www.awareparenting.com (advice/book orders)

Jackins' book is a classic text on what crying is and how to deal with it in both adults and children (background reading). Solter's draws on the same approach and is written for parents. Both take the approach that crying is an important release of distress (in both children and adults). These also help with our own reactions to our child's crying.

Other good sleep guides

Schaefer, CE and Petronko, MR: *Teach Your Baby to Sleep Through the Night.* Thorsons, 1989.This book is now out of print, but if you can get an old copy it is well worth reading. (The author's original bible!)

Hames, Penny: *Help Your Baby To Sleep,* Thorsons/NCT, 2002 (£6.99). A sound NCT review of baby sleep issues.

Key reference papers/surveys used by the author

ALSPAC 'Children of the Nineties' survey: Golding J, Pembrey M, Jones R, ALSPAC Study Team. ALSPAC – The Avon Longitudinal Study of Parents and Children. I. Study methodology. Paediatric and Perinatal Epidemiology 2001; 15:74–87. *website* www.alspac.bris.ac.uk/ALSPACext

Ball, HL: *Reasons to bed-share: why parents sleep with their infants,* (in press) Journal of Reproductive and Infant Psychology, 2002.

Nikolopoulou, M and St. James Roberts, I, *Preventing sleeping problems in infants who are at risk of developing them,* (in press) Archives of Disease in Childhood, 2002.

Morris, S, St. James Roberts I, et al: *Economic evaluation of strategies for managing crying and sleeping problems,* Archives of Disease in Childhood 2001;8415–19.

Ramchandi, P, Wiggs, L, et al: *A systematic review of treatments for settling problems and night waking in children.* BMJ, vol 320, p209, Jan 2000

Useful products guide

Baby Sleep Bags – prevent waking due to kicking off covers. For babies from newborn to 6 years. Kiddycare, 5 Abbeylands Road, Pluscarden, ELGIN IV30 8UB, Scotland (+44) (0)1343 890389.
Website www.kiddycarebabybags.com *e-mail* sales@kiddycarebabybags.com

Natural and organic mattresses and bedding – Willey Winkle, Offa House, Offa St., Hereford HR1 2LH, England (+44) (0)1432 268018
Website www.willeywinkle.co.uk

Sleeping Baby Products – including specially researched baby sleep and massage music CDs, nursery products, baby sleep books and more. Via web ordering only, email for full list of products:
Website www.babysleepguide.co.uk

Helpful organisations

Association for Post Natal Illness
145 Doors Road, Fulham, London SW6 7EB
(+44) (0)207 386 0868 (Mon/Wed/Fri, 10am–2pm; Tue/Thurs 10am–5pm)
This association offers one-to-one support to mothers suffering from post-natal-illness. See also MAMA, below.
Website www.apni.org   *e-mail* info@apni.org

Crysis
(+44) (0)207 404 5011
A self help/support organisation for families with excessively crying, sleepless and demanding babies. (A central telephone referral service refers you to your local telephone volunteer.)

Full Time Mothers
P.O. Box 186, London SW3 5RF
A national parent network and campaigning group for mothers (or fathers) who are at home caring for their children. Quarterly newsletter and meetings in London. See also WATCh?, below.
Website www.fulltimemothers.org
e-mail fulltimemothers@hotmail.com

Gingerbread
1st Floor, 7 Sovereign Close, Sovereign Ct, London E1W 3HW
Advice Line: (+44) (0)800 018 4318 (calls from UK free)
An organisation offering support, advice and friendship to lone parents. There is also a network of local support groups.
Website www.gingerbread.org.uk   *e-mail* office@gingerbread.org.uk

Hyperactive Children's Support Group (HACSG).
If you think your baby's sleep problems may be caused by diet or allergy, contact: HACSG, 71 Whyke Lane, Chichester, W. Sussex PO19 7PD, England
(+44) (0)1243 551313
Website www.hacsg.org.uk

Meet a Mum Association (MAMA)
Post-natal Depression Helpline (weekdays 7–10 pm): (+44) (0)1761 433598
Mama organises local groups offering support to mothers who feel isolated and to those who may be suffering from post-natal depression.
Website www.mama.org

National Childbirth Trust
Alexandra House, Oldham Terrace, Acton, London W3 6NH, England
Enquiries line: (+44) (0)870 4448707 (9am – 5pm)
Breastfeeding line: (+44) (0)870 4448708 (8am – 10pm; 7 days/week)
The NCT runs antenatal classes and provides information on maternity issues, breastfeeding and postnatal support including specialist groups for caesareans and miscarriage. It has 335 branches in the U.K.
Websites   www.nct-online.org   www.nctpregnancyandbabycare.com

NSPCC (National Society for Prevention of Cruelty to Children)
Freephone 24 hr Child Protection Helpline: (+44) (0)808 800 5000
Free leaflets from: (+44) (0)20 7825 2775
If you have any worries that stress caused by your crying child has led or might lead to shaking a baby or other violence in your home, this free 24 hour helpline provides confidential counselling and advice for those under stress.
Website   nspcc.org.uk (free literature is downloadable from the site).

Parent Line (Scotland) and Parentline Plus (rest of UK)
Helpline: (+44) (0)808 800 2222 – puts you through to the service in your area.
(Scottish hours: Mon/Wed/Fri, 9am–4pm; Tue/Thurs 3pm–9pm
24 hour service for rest of UK)
A family support service run by trained volunteers providing a helpline service for parents or carers experiencing problems connected with parenting children of all ages.
Websites   www.parentlineplus.org.uk   www.child1st.org.uk

Reciprocal Counselling (see Appendix 2)
For a list of local trainers/groups for adults wishing to improve their ability to handle crying/distress, write to/e-mail the head office in the U.S.A:
'Personal counsellor', 719, 2nd Avenue North, Seattle, Washington 98109, USA.
e-mail   ircc@rc.org

Relate
To find your local branch, look under 'Relate' in your telephone directory (England, Wales and N. Ireland), or under 'Couple Counselling' (Scotland). These organisations provide a confidential counselling service for anyone experiencing relationship difficulties.
Websites   www.relate.org.uk   www.couplecounselling.org

Sleep Scotland
(+44) (0)131 651 1392
Children with special needs –Scotland only
A charity offering sleep counselling to Scottish families whose children have special needs and sleep problems (usually for children 18 months +)
Website   www.sleepscotland.com
e-mail   sleepscotland@btinternet.com

The Foundation for the Study of Infant Death (FSID)
Artillery House, 11–19 Artillery Row, London SW1P 1RT
(+44) (0)207 233 2090
The Foundation can offer advice to those who are concerned about the safety of their baby during sleep times.
Website   www.sids.org.uk/fsid
e-mail   fsid@sids.org.uk

WATCh? (What about the Children?)
60 Bridge Street, Pershore, Worcs WR10 1AX
+44 (0)1386 561635
Website   www.whataboutthechildren.org.uk
e-mail   enquiries@whataboutthechildren.org.uk
A membership charity providing excellent literature about the emotional needs of young children. An excellent resource for mothers trying to make the decision about whether or not to go back to work, use childcare, etc.

Practitioner organisations

BioCare
Lakeside, 180 Lifford Lane, Kings Norton, Birmingham B30 3NU
Technical Support: +44 (0)121 433 8702
Sales Team: +44 (0)121 433 3727
Biocare offer a free telephone/email advice service staffed by qualified nutritional therapists and naturopaths who are happy to advise on infant and child nutritional supplements.
e-mail   technical@biocare.co.uk

British Association of Nutritional Therapy (BANT)
(+44) (0)870 6061284 (8.30am–6pm)
If you think that your child may be suffering from nutritional deficiency or food allergy, you can call this number to find out details of qualified local practitioners.
Website www.bant.org.uk

British Homeopathic Association
(+44) (0)207 566 7800
15 Clerkenwell Close, London EC1R 5AA
Send an SAE for a full list of GPs also trained in homeopathy, an information pack and NHS availability. Consulting an NHS homeopath is free.
Website www.trusthomeopathy.org

Recommended Radiesthetist (Section 7): Mr. A. Riggs
33 Parvills, Parklands Estate, Waltham Abbey, Essex EN9 1QG
Write with an SAE if you are concerned about electromagnetic or earth radiation affecting your child's sleeping place.

The British Society for Allergy, Environmental and Nutritional Medicine
P.O. Box 7, Knighton, LD7 1WT, England
Send a large SAE to this address for a list of private registered medical practitioners specialising in food/chemical allergy, intolerance &/or nutrition.

The General Osteopathic Council
(+44) (0)207 357 6655 ext. 242. If your baby is unsettled following a difficult birth, osteopathy may help to settle your child. Cranial osteopathy is especially gentle and of great value in the treatment of babies. There is a specialist Cranial Osteopathy enquiry line run by:

The Sutherland Society
Enquiry Line: (+44) (0)845 603 0680
15a Church Street, Bradford on Avon BA15 1LN.
The UK's largest cranial osteopathic organisation. Call for details of your nearest practitioner.
Website www.cranial.co.uk
email enquiries@churchstreetpractice.co.uk

The Institute for Complementary Medicine

(+44) (0)207 237 5165

· P.O. Box 194, London SE16 7QZ.

If you wish to obtain a full list of recognised complementary practitioners in the many different disciplines of complementary medicine near to you, please send an SAE and 2 loose stamps to this address.

Website   www.icmedicine.co.uk (practitioners are also listed on the website).

The International Association of Infant Massage (UK office)

56 Sparsholt Road, Barking, Essex IG11 7YQ

(+44) (0)7816 289788

Baby massage can help to relax babies as part of the pre-bed routine. This organisation will provide details of baby massage classes and qualified instructors near to you.

Website   www.iaim.org.uk

e-mail   mail@iaim.org.uk

The National Institute of Medical Herbalists

Medicinal herbal preparations for breast-feeding mothers can assist breast-milk production and positively affect the baby via the milk. Older babies and toddlers may be prescribed medicines directly.

56, Longbrook Street, Exeter, Devon EX4 6AH, England

(+44) (0)1392 426022

Website   www.nimh.org.uk

e-mail   nimh@UKexeter.freeserve.co.uk

Appendix 1
Weaning your baby off night feeds

Some health visitors recommend doing weaning and a sleep programme at the same time. This can be too much for baby and parent. I suggest doing weaning in two stages: the first stage, as part of your preparations for the sleep programme, is to dramatically reduce the amount of breast or formula milk (or other liquids) that your baby takes in at night. In this way, there will no longer be a physiological need for this once you start the sleep programme. The second stage will involve changing remaining patterns – the learned behaviour that a breast or bottle is needed to go to sleep, rather than whatever comes out of it!

By 6 months of age, unless your baby was very premature (in which case make allowances for this), almost all babies should be ready to give up night feeds. They are usually starting on solids anyway, and should therefore be ready for this.

Are you reluctant to finish night feeding?

Some breast-feeding mothers find it emotionally difficult to stop feeding at night. But by continuing to do so after this stage, you may be placing an unnecessary stress on the infant's digestive and urinary systems. Milk is a food, not a drink. Your baby's digestive system needs a rest at night rather than to be processing food and creating sodden nappies. Once night feeding is finished, your baby will begin to take in more calories during the day.

I know of cases where some have breast-fed their child several times throughout the night up to two years and older. If you are finding the thought of finishing night feedings difficult, it might be worth considering your motives for wanting to keep going. If it is because your child is reliant upon the breast in order to go back to sleep and you do not want her to cry, then read appendix 2 on crying. If it is because you sleep with your child and she is now in control of the feeding schedule, please re-read section 4. In this situation, you may be advised to re-consider whether your bed-sharing policy is the best one for your child at this present time. Is there a possibility that your enjoyment of breast-feeding has become a need for you yourself?

Using the following methods you should be able to eliminate night feeding within one to two weeks. The length of time that this stage takes will depend completely on how quickly you wish to reduce the quantities of milk/juice.

Preparatory actions (prior to the baby sleep programme)

1 Get your baby into her own cot
   Assuming you are reading this because you wish to carry out the baby sleep programme, your baby either is or will be in a cot. (Weaning off the breast whilst sleeping right next to your baby strikes me as nearly impossible!)

2 If *breast-feeding*: Richard Ferber recommends using a clock to check the duration of each feed
   • If it is a very brief comfort feed (less than one minute) then the baby is really not taking much milk and is just using you for comfort. You do not need to carry out any further preparation for a sleep programme on this score.
   • If the baby is taking in a significant amount of milk follow Instruction 4).

3 If *bottle-feeding*: follow Instruction 4

4 Reducing the amount of milk/liquid at night.
   This method is based on the one recommended by Richard Ferber. Each night reduce the amount of milk consumed at each feed by one fluid ounce (for bottle-feeding) and one minute (for breast-feeding). When you get to four fluid ounces of milk, you can either continue to reduce the amount or simply make the drink more and more dilute by adding less and less milk powder
   Note: Never vary the formula ratio like this during the day as milk is a food, but this can be very useful at night.

When you get to *one fluid ounce*, extremely *dilute milk* (almost water) or *one minute* of breastfeeding, you can proceed to the baby sleep programme. If your child was drinking juice at night, dilute the juice progressively (and reduce the amount of liquid if more than four fluid ounces) until it is almost water.

Completing night weaning during the baby sleep programme

Once you start the programme, drop the remaining token feed/s completely and use the checking procedure to deal with the baby's waking. Remember, once you start the sleep programme, you will be putting your child down to sleep *awake*. Once your child learns to put herself to sleep, eliminating any remaining night-time waking (due to needing the bottle or breast for going back to sleep) should be extremely quick, unless your baby was previously feeding very frequently during the night.

When you begin the checking procedure outlined on page 53, it is ideal if the parent who does *not* usually give the night feeds/drinks (usually the father) goes in for the checks instead of the mother at the time of the previous feed/drink. This will give a clear message to the baby that the previous feed is now no longer occurring and make it much easier on the mother if she was previously breast-feeding at this time. (It will also avoid the 'let-down' reflex enabling the baby to smell the milk from breast-feeding mothers.) Some parents offer water at this stage; but, provided your baby is taking drinks during the day and is not ill/feverish, she should get used to not drinking at all during the night.

If your baby was feeding extremely frequently during the night (say three or more times) then you may have trouble eliminating all the feeds simultaneously during a sleep programme. In this case, eliminate the earliest feeds first and then gradually eliminate the remaining early morning feeds one by one.

Appendix 2
Understanding and coping with crying

I would follow a baby sleep programme, but I am simply not willing to let my baby cry, even for half a minute, is sometimes the response to the suggestions in this guide.

> At 9 months old our child Boris used to wake up five to six times a night. Despite wanting to, I had never managed to try the techniques in the guide as my wife Ana thought they would be ineffective and that the idea of leaving our baby to cry even for short periods sounded cruel. But your guide persuaded her and our son now sleeps through without waking. Our family's health and balance has improved greatly as a result of your book.
>
> *Dejan Deletic, Aberdeen*

Many parents become extremely distressed themselves about the idea of having to listen to their baby's crying without doing something apart from checking every few minutes. *If I could understand why the crying doesn't hurt him,* one mother said, *it would make things much easier for me.* That is the aim of this section.

Obviously, the ideal scenario would be for your baby to learn to gradually put himself back to sleep, with a minimum of complaint, from the early weeks onwards. Of course you do not want to cause your baby distress. Many parents who observe the preventive principles with their younger babies outlined in Section 3 will achieve a good sleep pattern for their baby without him needing to cry at all.

However, if your baby is 6 months old or more and has acquired very strong habits (sleep associations) of needing your help to go to sleep, and of crying to get your response, then he needs help to unlearn both of these habits. While he is learning the new habits, he may cry more than usual. If you do not allow him to cry once he gets to this stage, he may not be able to change the these habits.

In this appendix, we will look at:

- Why is my baby crying during the sleep programme?
- How can I keep night crying to a minimum?
- Could crying have long-term effects on my baby?
- Why is it so hard for me to hear my baby crying?
- How can I cope better with the crying during the programme?

1 Why is my baby crying during the sleep programme?

Your baby is crying as a result of the sleep programme for two main reasons:

- because he may have been inadvertently trained to cry by you, his carer.
- because his crying helps him to discharge his distress at not getting what he wants

The way that you may have trained him to cry is that, previously, as soon as he has cried, you have responded with whatever it is that he associates with going (back) to sleep, whether it be milk, physical contact or any other routine. So he is used to getting an instant response to a cry. Initially, he will keep crying in order to elicit that same response – he may even cry harder and harder to get this. He will also be upset about the change in policy, and upset that his usual 'sleep associations' are not forthcoming.

You are checking him to reassure him that you are still there and that you love him. However, you are not picking him up or giving him what he previously relied upon, in order to give him a clear message that 'night-time is for sleeping – we are not going to have milk, stroking, etc., at night any more'. You are also giving him the opportunity to learn how to put himself back to sleep.

2   How can I keep night crying to a minimum?

There may be other reasons why a baby may need to cry at night in addition to the cries which are specifically in response to a sleep programme. It is important to understand the difference between these two reasons, so that these other upsets can be dealt with, thus reducing the level of crying generally.

If you have not already weaned your baby off night feeds, please turn to appendix 1 and follow those instructions before you start the baby sleep programme. This will ensure that any crying during the programme is kept to a minimum.

First, remember the various reasons why your baby might be distressed in the night, (we are assuming that he is not hungry):

- He may be over-stimulated – the day has been too hectic and confusing
- He is remembering past distress, including birth trauma
- He may be suffering from extra separation anxiety (usually at 10 months or slightly earlier), perhaps brought on by you going back to work or some other reason

All of these possible tensions can be 'discharged' by crying. The simple philosophy that 'distress' (which is tension or upset) can be eliminated or 'discharged' by crying, ideally in the presence of a loving person, comes from the field of Reciprocal Counselling. This very simple and practical branch of psychotherapy has been of huge value to me in my understanding of how to deal with my own children's crying – as well as my own response to it – and I fully encourage any reader to find out more about it (see the Help Section).

> The great majority of lullaby lyrics contain the words such as: 'Don't cry'. Yet if we allow our child to cry when he needs to get rid of tension, he will be much more settled overall.

If you allow your child to fully discharge his tensions in the daytime, he is much less likely to cry at night. (See also the advice in Section 3, Key 6.) If, when your child cries in the day, you cannot find any obvious cause (such as pain, hunger, wet nappy, tiredness etc.), I suggest you just hold your baby and allow him to discharge distress without distracting him from it. By allowing this, you can be surer that during a sleep programme crying is only related to that immediate moment and not to a need to discharge past events.

> Do not always respond to daytime cries with food, rocking, dummies, etc. If we do this, we teach our child that it is 'not OK to cry', and make it more likely that he will become dependent upon the things which suppress his crying.

If you have just started work, see Appendix 5 for some suggestions on how to make sure that you get some regular, relaxed quality time with your baby, who may, quite simply, be crying because he is missing you.

Crying (day or night-time), as we have seen, may also be connected to the infant's need to discharge a frightening birth memory or other *past* experience. If he is never allowed to cry during the day, night-time may be the only time he gets to release these tensions.

Although reciprocal counsellors believe that, to be truly therapeutic, crying should be witnessed by someone else, this is not fully possible during a sleep programme because the presence of the parent would clearly be counterproductive to learning a new pattern of behaviour and the release of tension associated with it. However, as long as your child feels safe and comforted (by his comfort object and also by your regular checks) I believe he can still discharge by crying at night, with no ill effects.

3   Could crying have long-term effects on my baby?

As long as your baby is weaned, physically healthy and you have a normal bond of love with him, there is no risk in allowing him to cry at night during a sleep programme.

Why sleep programmes are not harmful:

- They have been repeatedly proven in University studies to produce no long term ill effects in babies
- They are the method of choice for hospital sleep clinics and leading sleep experts

● Even those babies who cry for quite long periods will usually wake happily the next morning

When I was carrying out a sleep programme with my children, they would always wake extremely happy the next morning, despite being allowed to cry the night before (with me checking them regularly) and I was unable to detect any negative effect whatsoever. This experience is mirrored by many other parents who have used these techniques.

4   Why is it so hard to hear my baby crying?

Parents have 'stored distress' too – which can include memories of previous painful experiences of our own. One reason we are generally not keen to listen to our baby's crying, is because it reminds us of (or 'restimulates') previous painful experiences of our own. This brings up the conditioned urge to suppress the pain – usually because we ourselves were told: 'Don't cry' as children. So this gives us the urge to stop our own babies and children crying at all costs. It is important that we become able *calmly* to 'witness' the daytime crying of our babies when necessary and also to allow night-time crying to continue for short periods during a sleep programme.

Other reasons may be that:

● you have been working so hard since your baby was born to minister to his every need that it goes against your previous experience and (wrongly) makes you feel as if you are being negligent
● neighbours, friends and family may (wrongly) tell you that you are cruel
● you worry (unnecessarily) that the crying during the programme must be a result of some deep-seated need rather than the breaking of habits

With respect to the last point, if you allow sufficient day-time crying, as well as sufficient contact time in the day, you are ensuring that the night-time crying is not the result of a deep-seated need that you would be wrong to ignore.

5   How can I cope better with the crying during the programme?

If you are finding the crying too distressing, you do not have to listen to your baby's crying if you do not want to once you have done your quick check (as long as you know he has no way of being hurt in the cot and you are assured of his safety), and you must not feel guilty. The stress you are feeling will only have further negative effects upon you. (If you are concerned about vomiting (see page 62) then it is important for one partner to listen out).

Some of the following are suggested in the literature:

- remove yourself out of earshot for the 5–20 minute period before the next quick check;
- put some 'white noise' on to mask the crying (TV between channels, hairdryer, etc.);
- put on some soothing music.

Appendix 3

An alternative sleep programme – the graded leaving approach

There are various situations for which this alternative technique is recommended:

- if you have had difficulty in allowing your child to cry during the programme
- if you have had her in bed with you since birth for an extended period
- if she is over 10 months and suffers extreme separation anxiety during the day
- if she suffers from severe asthma or eczema
- if she vomits twice or more as a reaction to the standard programme

In the first two points, your child will have had very little experience of either being left or of crying. In this case, her reaction to the initial changes in the leaving/checking approach described as part of the baby sleep programme may be too distressing, certainly for you as parents. In these situations, sleep therapists find that this graded approach is the only acceptable option for certain situations. However, as long as your baby is in good health, you are strongly advised to use the main technique described in this book if at all possible. Many parents get fed up with the slower progress of this method and eventually opt for the main method anyway.

The basic idea of this alternative method is to very gently wean a baby off the need for your presence for going to sleep, in very gradual stages. After putting your baby in the cot, you slowly move away, and out of the room. But consistency is still crucial and it is still necessary to observe certain rules and procedures, such as not picking the baby up when she cries for you.

Possible disadvantages of the graded approach

- It is much slower and may take weeks to achieve.
- You may get 'stuck' in one part of it (e.g. whereas before you lay on your child's bed each night for protracted periods, you may find that you get stuck with sitting on a chair at your child's door for the same length of time!).
- Depending on the child, it may still involve allowing your child to cry, albeit with you present or nearby.
- It may make the night-time checking routine much more drawn out and exhausting for parents.

Steps to follow

1 For the first 3 nights, sit near (not on) your baby's bed or cot until she falls asleep. Do not touch or stroke her. Continue to observe the other principles within the baby sleep programme (i.e. not picking baby up if she cries etc.). Tell your baby that she will soon be able to sleep without your help, and say 'Go to sleep' in a firm, positive voice. Then remain silent. If there is crying, you can repeat the instruction at intervals.

2 For the next 3 nights, move your chair a few feet from the bed (very gradually); or

3 Move your chair to the doorway for the following 3 nights and repeat the same positive message that she soon won't need you to go to sleep.

4 Go further and further away in 3 nightly stages – outside the door, down the hall, down the stairs.

5 When your child cries out for you – *don't go to the bedside.* Just say 'Go back to sleep' as before. Do not get upset or show too much concern.

6 If you wish, you can pretend to be asleep and close your eyes, and remain as calm and undisturbed as possible (since your distress will re-stimulate the baby's).

Dealing with night crying using the graded approach

Ideally you should still not go in straight away. Follow the same checking procedure already described, but rather than returning to bed after checking the baby and telling her to go to sleep, replicate putting her to bed in the first place by taking yourself back to the *last position you sat in when she went to sleep at bedtime;* and if necessary, at intervals, repeat the reassurance: 'Go back to sleep, Mummy/Daddy is here', etc.

Appendix 4

Allergy, deficiency and diet in connection with baby sleep problems

The lack of UK studies on the possible link between diet and infant sleep has led some national experts to conclude that there is no link at all, despite convincing evidence from studies on older children. However, other experts do acknowledge a link, and evidence from the USA plus information collected by the UK charity The Hyperactive Children's Support Group (HACSG) has certainly convinced me that if your baby has several of the symptoms in the check list on page 40 you would do well to take action. Certainly, if the response to the baby sleep programme is poor, he could either be reacting to certain foodstuffs and/or be deficient in key nutrients.

Adverse reactions to foods and nutritional deficiencies often tend to go hand-in-hand, and there can be family tendencies to food allergies. One study on infants under one year old with a history of both allergy and sleep problems, quoted by Schaefer and Petronko, found that when cow's milk products were removed from the diet, the average night sleep increased from four and a half to over ten hours per night. One paediatrician in Portland, Oregon, Dr. Joseph T. Hart, found that babies who woke habitually many times in the night would begin sleeping through until morning just with the addition of zinc supplements. Deficiencies of essential fatty acids are also implicated.

Allergy and Attention Deficit Hyperactivity Disorder (ADHD)

1 in 200 children is thought to be affected by allergy and hyperactivity (ADHD). A list of symptoms has been identified which characterise children with this syndrome. In babies and infants, 60 percent of those with this syndrome were found to wake five or more times at night (the other symptoms are listed in the

check list on page 40). In older children, sleeplessness is a well-documented symptom of food allergy and hyperactivity. Other symptoms include: clumsiness, aggression, impulsiveness, disruptiveness, poor co-ordination, unnatural strength, learning difficulties, argumentativeness and aggression. More boys than girls have this syndrome.

Mothers of these children and other family members often suffer from: migraine, hay fever, rhinitis, arthritis, asthma or eczema, and the mother may have suffered from poor nutrition, severe stress, allergy or illness during pregnancy.

If you wish to get a diagnosis for this syndrome, do speak to your doctor; however, as many GPs are not familiar with experts on this syndrome, you may wish to consult with someone with specialist knowledge in this field. You could consult privately with a specialist medical practitioner listed by the British Society for Allergy, Environmental and Nutritional Medicine (BANT) or someone recommended by the HCSG, who also provide literature and advice on dietary change. You may be encouraged to omit all cow's-milk- based dairy products and various other foodstuffs from the baby's and/or your own diet (since substances may pass through in breast milk) for a period of time and then to re-introduce them one at a time, being extremely careful to include nutritionally adequate substitutes for an infant. You may also be prescribed food supplements.

Nutritional deficiencies and food supplements

It is possible that your baby's sleep is being affected by purely nutritional deficiency, even if ADHD is not present. If during the pregnancy the mother has been deficient in minerals or essential fatty acids, for example, the developing foetus may inherit such deficiencies.

> You should seek professional advice before supplementing the diet of a very young child.

BANT provides a list of nutritional therapists throughout the U.K. and you should aim to consult one of these. However, if this is not possible, the supplement company, BioCare (see Practitioner List), have created excellent infant formulae which are approved for babies of 3 months and over and which may well help with unsettled, sleepless or colicky babies. You can speak to one of their nutritional therapist advisors free of charge by telephone. Remember, it is always best to improve diet (a breast-feeding mother's as well as the baby's) rather than just giving a baby supplements.

If you decide to give your baby food supplements:

- do so with professional advice;
- always follow the recommended doses on the products;
- remember that: any decisions to supplement the diet of a young child are taken at your own risk.

Cow's milk formula – bottle fed babies

If your baby is bottle-fed and seems to suffer from the symptoms on page 40, is very 'colicky' or has an intractable sleep problem, talk to your doctor or health visitor about using a goat milk or soya-based infant formula instead. One study found that 15 out of 17 babies with sleep problems for which no other cause could be found, slept normally after cow's milk formula was removed.

Intolerances to foods – babies on solids

If your child does not fit the ADHD picture, but you are still concerned to eliminate any possibility of reactions or intolerances to foods, then you may also wish to seek specialist help, although it is possible to experiment at home with the suggestions below. The items listed below are most commonly involved in food allergy and intolerance in infants. Experts recommend removing them *for a period of at least two weeks* and charting any effect upon sleep. My advice is that if you cannot omit all the following simultaneously, then start with cow's dairy products.

N.B. Many mothers are encouraged to introduce solid food – in my opinion far too early on. Babies only just onto solid food do not need extra dairy products (such as yoghurt or fromage frais) in addition to their breast or formula milk feeds – there are plenty of other non-dairy food options (especially rice, fruit and vegetable- based foodstuffs) which are adequate at this age.

- **Dairy products** These include milk, cream, yoghurt, cheese, butter, ice-cream, and milk chocolate. Watch labels for whey, curd, lactose, caseinates –

for example, many margarines contain whey. Substitutes are: soya, oat or rice milk, whey-free margarines, soya ice-cream (now in most supermarkets) and soya yoghurts and desserts (from health food shops). Also obviously omit cow's milk infant formula. If this change has a beneficial effect, you can try initially introducing goat and sheep's milk products (which will allow you to have milk and yoghurt) and see if the results are maintained;

- **Sugar and chocolate** (including non-milk chocolate);
- **Additives** and artificial colourings, flavour enhancers (like monosodium glutamate) and artificial sweeteners (such as aspartame);
- **Oranges and orange juice;**
- **Eggs and nuts;**
- **Wheat** (try oat and rice-based products instead of rusks, bread and wheat-based breakfast cereals).

If you feel that to do all the above is too large or sudden a change, try first eliminating all *dietary* cow's milk products followed later by changing the cow's *formula milk* if necessary as a further measure. The HCSG also recommend filtering tap water (as well as the usual boiling and cooling), using a jug filter. Remember to change the filter cartridges regularly.

If you notice a beneficial effect, then gradually re-introduce the products (to your baby's or your own diet) and note any changes. *Note: Changes may take a few days to manifest and may reoccur gradually. If the symptoms recur, omit the foods again in turn.*

Remember that sleep problems may be a combination of dietary *and* behavioural factors – even if your child is allergic, you may still have to carry out the changes in Sections 5 and 6!

Appendix 5
For mothers who work outside the home

My first baby never slept more than four consecutive hours at night until she was three and a half years old. I was working full time and in order to function at work I kept blankets in my car to use for naps in the day. I actually put off having my second child because of the dread of it happening again. Too busy with work to share experiences with other parents, I had no idea why I had a problem. The information in your book filled that gap and showed me my fundamental mistake: my mother and the nanny who provided daycare had been rocking and feeding my baby to sleep so she expected the same from me at night.

Maria, Telecommunications executive, London

Many mothers are understandably desperate to get their babies to 'sleep through' early on because of the pressure to return to full-time work outside the home when their baby is still very young – often before the baby is physically ready to sleep through. This section aims to give practical advice to assist good night-time sleep for those who are both still trying to decide whether to return to work and to those who have already made the decision to do so.

Still trying to choose whether to 'go back'?

Even though surveys show that the majority of women prefer to work part-time while their babies are very small, or to work from home, workplace pressures mean that not everyone has the option to do so. As a result there are large numbers of mothers with small babies in full-time work outside the home, only a small percentage of whom are completely happy with this situation.

It may seem to go against the political correctness of the day, but the reality is that mothers (who are also the only ones able to breastfeed) are generally the main carers of small babies. Both research and my personal experience have convinced me that if the main carer spends the majority of her time with the baby for at least the first six months of the baby's life, the baby is better off, happier and more settled. Families where mothers can stay at home longer, (or where the baby can be cared for at home by the father, another close relative or a full-time nanny) – do not undergo the sudden changes to developing or established day and night routines of breast-feeding, naps and night-time care which can occur when Mum returns to work. They also avoid confusing their baby with a possible clash between different home and non-home routines (i.e. where a baby goes to a day-care centre).

As every mother knows, motherhood is a full-time job in itself! Although this valuable work is often seen as having a lower status than paid employment, there is a new move to support 'at home mothers' in viewing their decision as a positive, life-enriching experience, rather than in any way less important or a retrograde career move. The Full Time Mothers group is one network and campaign group (see Help Section) which exists to support parents making the choice to stay at home with their children. The charity What About The Children? (WATCh?) offers excellent literature packs which provide authoritative, independent research evidence on the emotional needs of very young children, as well as information on childcare, etc.

Making your work a positive choice ...

However, if you are returning to work soon out of choice or necessity, try to embrace the decision positively and not let stress or guilt upset the atmosphere at home. Here are some extra tips to help this transition go smoothly.

1   Get your baby into good routines early on

As we have already seen, some experts see no problem in starting to use some of the techniques in this guide earlier than 6 months, in order to encourage a younger baby into independent sleep as soon as possible. However, please be realistic about what your very young baby is capable of and read Section 3 carefully.

2   Match day-care to home-care

Make sure that whoever is looking after your baby in the daytime is aware of your outlook and approach, for example making sure that your baby is put down to sleep awake for daytime sleeps. If you are following the sleep programme in this guide, it would be ideal if those in charge of day-care could also be shown this guide.

3   Don't let guilt make you inconsistent

There is one major factor to consider which may well affect how both you behave at night with your baby – and that is any guilt you feel about working in the daytime.

> With my first baby I found it impossible to put a sleep programme into operation as I felt incredibly guilty if I heard him cry at night and would respond immediately to all cries. This was mainly because I was back at work and worried that he was crying for me in the night because he was missing me in the day.
>
> *Vanessa Impey, medical student, Glasgow*

Any guilt you feel may affect your ability to be consistent at night. Some working mothers choose to bed-share because they are away from their child in the day. If you do this, that is your decision and a valid one. However, what is not ideal is to chop and change policies on a daily basis: sometimes taking her into your bed when she wakes at night and other times leaving her to cry. Lack of consistency is not fair on your baby and will cause problems.

4   Spend some quality time together every day

If you are always rushing home at night, stressed and tired, in order to spend quality time with your baby before bedtime – or even asking for your tired and grizzly baby to be kept awake in order to see you – that is obviously not ideal. In this situation, consider setting aside half an hour or so in the early morning, before work, as the time to have with your baby. However, if you can easily manage to be at home in the evening, then make the pre-bed routine your quality time together.

> I work long hours five days a week. My 10-month-old son used to constantly whimper for my attention in the evenings. Things have got a lot better now that I spend more quality time with him before bedtime: playing for a while in his bedroom after the last feed. Then I sing a lullaby and cuddle him for a while and then just when his eyes start to close, I put him into his cot and as a result we have far fewer problems at bedtime.
>
> *Stephanie Simmons, Computer Analyst, Ireland*

5   Don't start a sleep programme just when you're returning to work

A sleep programme may be less likely to work if the child is simultaneously adapting to a new sleep programme, new day-care, less time with his main carer and other new changes in routine. Be aware that his sleep patterns may be affected by your return to work, and let him adapt to the new situation before commencing the programme in sections 5 and 6. It is best to plan for your return over the few weeks before, rather than rushing into a sleep programme at short notice.

Babies need fathers too!

Even if the mother is at home, remember that babies also like to see their working fathers. Some may be reluctant to go to sleep until Dad has come home from work. If the mother is working out of the home it is obviously a great alternative if the father can manage the bed-time routine instead.

Matthew had never slept through the night since he was born and would often wait up for his father to come home from work late. I would try to put him down at 9 pm but would find him playing with toys at midnight. By the age of three, health visitors reported that his lack of sleep was affecting his growth and development. I attended my local sleep clinic and was helped to develop a strategy for getting Matthew to bed at 7 pm every night. We persevered and after three weeks he suddenly decided that when the clock pointed to the top it was bedtime. Matthew is now much happier and putting on weight.

Jane, Wiltshire

SLEEP DIARY	DAY BEFORE PROGRAMME Date:	DAY ONE Date:	DAY TWO Date:	DAY THREE Date:
BED-TIME Time routine began				
Time put to bed				
Length of time until asleep				
Times of checks (if applicable)				
NIGHT-TIME Times of night-waking, night checks and other details				
DAY-TIME Time of waking in the morning				
Fed immediately or gradual delay?				
Mood on waking				
Lengths and times of daytime sleeps				

SLEEP DIARY	DAY FOUR Date:	DAY FIVE Date:	DAY SIX Date:	DAY SEVEN Date:
BED-TIME Time routine began				
Time put to bed				
Length of time until asleep				
Times of checks (if applicable)				
NIGHT-TIME Times of night-waking, night checks and other details				
DAY-TIME Time of waking in the morning				
Fed immediately or gradual delay?				
Mood on waking				
Lengths and times of daytime sleeps				

You are advised to use pencil to allow re-use. Photocopying breaches copyright.

Celebrating Christmas Together

*Nativity and Three Kings Plays
with Stories and Songs*

Estelle Bryer and Janni Nicol

Create the wonder of Christmas with your children at school or at home – starting with a simple Advent Calendar and Crib Scene. *The Nativity Play* is spell binding – whether told as a story in verse, narrated whilst children act the parts or performed entirely by children. This Christmas treasury includes: the Nativity Play with staging directions and instructions for simple costumes and props; songs and music to accompany the play; how to create a Crib scene; making an Advent Calendar; the Three Kings Play and Christmas stories.

96pp; 210 x 148mm; 1 903458 20 X; paperback

Christmas Stories Together

Estelle Bryer and Janni Nicol

Here is a treasure trove of 36 tales for children aged 3–9. The stories range from Advent through Christmas ending with the Holy Family's flight into Egypt – in fact, tales for the whole year. These stories will soon become family favourites, with their imaginative yet down to earth language and lively illustrations.

'This book is alight with the genius of storytelling. It tenderly shows how to weave a pattern of stories over Advent and the twelve days of Christmas.'
  Nancy Mellon, author of Storytelling with Children

128pp; 210 x 148mm; 1 903458 22 6; paperback

The Genius of Play
Celebrating the spirit of childhood
Sally Jenkinson

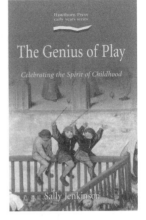

Children move like quick fire from the fantastic to the everyday, when free to express the genius of play. *The Genius of Play* addresses what play is, why it matters, and how modern life endangers children's play.

The secrets of play are explored from moving stories and research. Here is an outspoken Children's Play Charter for parents and teachers, which celebrates the playful spirit of childhood.

'A beautiful and important book.'

Mary Jane Drummond, University of Cambridge

'Offers much help to adults struggling to understand the power of play.'

Joan Almon, Co-chair,
Waldorf Early Childhood Association of North America

224pp; 216 x 138mm; 1 903458 04 8; paperback

Ready to Learn
From birth to school readiness
Martyn Rawson and Michael Rose

When are children ready for school? Many parents have concerns about their children entering formal schooling too early. They question the 'hot housing' of their children, and the accompanying stressful side-effects of 'too much formal schooling too soon'. *Ready to Learn* will help you to decide when your child is ready to take the step from kindergarten to school proper. The key is an imaginative grasp of how children aged 0–6 years learn to play, speak, think and relate between birth and six years of age.

'Readable, informative and thought provoking - pushes at the edge of contemporary ideas on readiness in a stimulating way ...'

John Burnett, BA (Hons), Waldorf Steiner Education,
Programme Director, Rolle School of Education, University of Plymouth

192pp; 216 x 138mm; 1 903458 15 3; paperback

Pull the Other One!
String Games and Stories Book 1
Michael Taylor

This well-travelled and entertaining series of tales is accompanied by clear instructions and explanatory diagrams – guaranteed not to tie you in knots and will teach you tricks with which to dazzle your friends! With something for everyone, these ingenious tricks and tales are developed and taught with utter simplicity, making them suitable from age 5 upwards.

'When we go wrong playing Cat's Cradle, we call it Dog's Cradle!'

Megan Gain, aged 6, London

128pp; 216 x 138mm; 1 869890 49 3; paperback

Now You See It ...
String Games and Stories Book 2
Michael Taylor

String games are fun, inviting children to exercise skill, imagination and teamwork. They give hands and fingers something clever and artistic to do! Following the success of *Pull the Other One!*, here are more of Michael Taylor's favourite string games, ideal for family travel, for creative play and for party tricks.

'Another gem from Hawthorn Press – an excellent book. Children can school their fine motor skills and co-ordination too. Michael's book introduces the other ingredient of healthy development: narrative, string games that tell stories!'

Martyn Rawson, Steiner Waldorf Schools Fellowship

136pp; 216 x 148mm; 1 903458 21 8; paperback

Sound Sleep
Calming and helping your baby or child to sleep
Sarah Woodhouse

Babies are wonderful, especially when they are happy and sleep well! However, many babies and young children get upset and cry for long periods for whatever reason and seem unable, as they get older, to sleep through the night. Some may cry and scream so often to get attention or ease the stress of colic or another discomfort, that exhausted parents are driven to distraction and despair. Yet most babies' distress and sleep problems can be solved once parents discover the particular ways which prove helpful. This comprehensive guide will help you make those discoveries. The step-by-step method of Timed Settling is an especially effective way for desperate parents to help their babies over nine months, toddlers and young children to learn to settle themselves and sleep through the night without disturbance.

'I wish I had seen this book when I became pregnant. I would have been prepared for anything – even the worst! The best thing about it is that it helps you to stay calm and try out new ways of coping. Some of the ideas did wonders for me.'   *Ruth, a 29-year-old mother*

128pp; 246 x 189mm; 1 903458 27 7; paperback

Storytelling with Children
Nancy Mellon

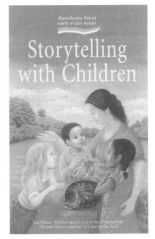

Telling stories awakens wonder and creates special occasions with children, whether it is bedtime, around the fire or on rainy days. Nancy Mellon shows how you can become a confident storyteller and enrich your family with the power of story.

'Nancy Mellon continues to be an inspiration for storytellers old and new. Her experience, advice and suggestions work wonders. They are potent seeds that give you the creative confidence to find your own style of storytelling.'

Ashley Ramsden, Director of the School of Storytelling, Emerson College

192pp; 216 x 138mm; 1 903458 08 0; paperback

Festivals, Family and Food
Guide to Seasonal Celebration
Diana Carey and Judy Large

This family favourite is a unique, well loved source of stories, recipes, things to make, activities, poems, songs and festivals. Each festival such as Christmas, Candlemas and Martinmas has its own, well illustrated chapter. There are also sections on Birthdays, Rainy Days, Convalescence and a birthday Calendar. The perfect present for a family, it explores the numerous festivals that children love celebrating.

'It's an invaluable resource book'

The Observer

'Every family should have one'

Daily Mail

224pp; 250 x 200mm; 0 950 706 23 X; paperback

Festivals Together
A Guide to Multicultural Celebration
Sue Fitzjohn, Minda Weston and Judy Large

This special book for families and teachers helps you celebrate festivals from cultures from all over the world. This resource guide for celebration introduces a selection of 26 Buddhist, Christian, Hindu, Jewish, Muslim and Sikh festivals. It offers a lively introduction to the wealth of different ways of life. There are stories, things to make, recipes, songs, customs and activities for each festival, comprehensively illustrated. You will be able to share in the adventures of Anancy the spider trickster, how Ganesh got his elephant head and share in Eid, Holi, Wesak, Advent, Divali, Chinese New Year and more.

'The ideal book for anyone who wants to tackle multicultural festivals'

Nursery World

224pp; 250 x 200mm; 1 869 890 46 9; paperback

Getting in touch with Hawthorn Press

We would be delighted to hear your feedback on our books, how they can be improved, and what your needs are. Visit our website for details of forthcoming books and events at www.hawthornpress.com

Ordering books

If you have difficulty ordering Hawthorn Press books from a bookshop, you can order direct from:

United Kingdom

Booksource
32 Finlas Street, Glasgow G22 5DU
Tel: 0141 558 1366   Fax: 0141 557 0189
E-mail: orders@booksource.net
Website: www.booksource.net

North America

SteinerBooks c/o Books International
PO Box 960, Herndon, VA 201 72-0960
Toll-free order line: 800-856-8664
Toll-free fax line: 800-277-9747

If you wish to follow up your reading of this book, please tick the boxes below as appropriate, fill in your name and address, and return it to

Hawthorn Press, Hawthorn House, 1 Lansdown Lane, Stroud, Glos GL5 1BJ, UK

or fax it to (+44) (0)1453 751138

☐ Please send me a catalogue of other Hawthorn Press books

☐ Please send me details of other Essential Health Guides

Name . . . .

Address . . . .

. . . .

Postcode . . . . Tel. no. . . . .